Englisch

8.-10. Klasse

If-Clauses & Co.

Englisch

8.-10. Klasse

In der neuen Rechtschreibung

Achim Groß

If-Clauses & Co. Die Nebensätze

(Subordinate Clauses)

In der Reihe FALKEN Schülerhilfe sind zahlreiche Titel erschienen.
Bitte fragen Sie in Ihrer Buchhandlung.

Der Text dieses Buches entspricht den Regeln der neuen deutschen Rechtschreibung.

Dieses Buch wurde auf chlorfrei gebleichtem und säurefreiem Papier gedruckt.

Die Deutsche Bibliothek – CIP-Einheitsaufnahme

Gross, Achim:
If-Clauses & Co. : die Nebensätze (subordinate clauses) ;
8. – 10. Klasse / Achim Gross. – Niedernhausen/Ts. : FALKEN, 1997
    (Schülerhilfe : Englisch)
    ISBN 3-8068-1784-7

ISBN 3 8068 1784 7

Umschlaggestaltung: Peter Udo Pinzer
Gestaltung: Horst Bachmann
Redaktion: Dr. Petra Begemann
Herstellung: Jürgen Domke
Titelgrafiken: Jovica Savin, Frankfurt am Main
Fotos: Archiv für Kunst und Geschichte, Berlin: 83; **Britische Zentrale für Fremdenverkehr,** Frankfurt am Main:
5, 45, 47, 50, 51; **dpa,** Frankfurt am Main: 21 oben; **FALKEN Archiv:** 29 unten links (H. Nadolny), 33 oben (TLC),
59 (W. Zöltsch), 64 (S. Layda); **Bildagentur Huber,** Garmisch-Partenkirchen: 29 unten rechts (P. J. Sharpe),
35 oben; **The Image Bank,** München: 23 oben (R. Lockyer), 29 oben links (K. Chernush), 29 Mitte rechts
(G. + M. D. de Lossy), 32 oben (B. Mitchell), 37 (N. Mareschal); **Gisela Kelbert,** Idstein: 33 unten, 39, 42;
KEYSTONE Pressedienst GmbH, Hamburg: 58, 71, 73, 78 oben; **Deutsche Lufthansa AG, PR-Bildstelle,**
Köln: 67 (oben: G. Rebenich, unten: A. Böttcher); **Ulrich Niehoff,** Bienenbüttel: 43; **Philips GmbH/Presse-
archiv:** 78 unten, 79; **Reinhard-Tierfoto,** Heiligkreuzsteinach: 25, 60; **Silvestris Fotoservice,** Kast/Obb.: 29 oben
rechts (Dietrich), 32 unten (J. Neuhaus), 34 oben (The Daily Telegraph Library), 34 unten (Uselmann),
48 (Craddock), 69 (Heine); **Sport-Presse-Fotos Wilfried Witters,** Hamburg: 17, 21 unten, 23 unten, 35 unten
Zeichnungen: Jovica Savin, Frankfurt am Main

Die Ratschläge in diesem Buch sind von dem Autor und vom Verlag sorgfältig erwogen und geprüft, dennoch
kann eine Garantie nicht übernommen werden. Eine Haftung des Autors bzw. des Verlags und seiner Beauftrag-
ten für Personen-, Sach- und Vermögensschäden ist ausgeschlossen.

Satz: Raasch & Partner GmbH, Neu-Isenburg
Druck: Ludwig Auer GmbH, Donauwörth

817 2635 4453 6271

INHALT

KEINE NEBENSACHE

··

Die Nebensätze: Einführung

Hallo, hier ist MacCool. Ich werde dir bei der Arbeit mit diesem Buch helfen. Immer wenn es schwierig wird, stehe ich dir mit Rat und Tat zur Seite.

Was verbirgt sich eigentlich hinter dem Titel „If-clauses & Co."? Nun natürlich, wie der Titel schon sagt, alles Wissenswerte zu den If-clauses, die du bestimmt aus dem Englischunterricht kennst. Aber es werden dir auch die weiteren Nebensatzarten im Englischen vorgestellt und erklärt – seien es nun der einfache Adverbialsatz, der Relativsatz oder die Nebensätze, die durch Partizipien ausgedrückt werden. Du siehst, es kommt eine Menge Interessantes auf dich zu.

Arten von Nebensätzen

Nebensätze sind dir sicherlich aus dem Deutschen bekannt. Wie könnte man ansonsten Wünsche, Begründungen oder nähere Erläuterungen zu Wörtern oder Satzteilen formulieren? Ich werde dich in diesem Zusammenhang häufig auf Gemeinsamkeiten und Unterschiede zwischen der deutschen und englischen Grammatik hinweisen, so dass bestimmt nicht alles, was du in diesem Buch erfährst, völlig neu für dich sein wird.

Die Zeichensetzung

Du hast dir bestimmt auch schon oft die Frage gestellt, wann denn nun im Englischen Kommas gesetzt werden. Im ersten Kapitel erkläre ich dir die englische Zeichensetzung und die Unterschiede zum Deutschen. Du kannst die Zeichensetzung ständig beim Durcharbeiten der Lernhilfe üben, so dass du zum Schluss auch in dieser Disziplin zu den Besten gehörst.

Wer das Buch benutzen sollte?

Wer kann üben?

Alle Schüler und Schülerinnen der Klassen 8 bis 10, aber auch diejenigen der Oberstufe, die noch einmal die Nebensätze wiederholen möchten. Mit Hilfe dieses Buches könnt ihr selbständig Unsicherheiten im Gebrauch der Nebensätze beheben.

Wie das Buch aufgebaut ist?

Du findest in dieser Lernhilfe übersichtliche Regelkästen mit vielen Beispielen und Übungen dazu, die in „A" (leicht) und „B" (schwieriger) unterteilt sind. Auf der Randspalte sind die Regeln noch einmal kurz zusammengefasst, damit du sie dir besser einprägen kannst. Jedes Kapitel endet mit Abschlusstests, die dir zeigen, ob du alles verstanden hast.

Regeln und Übungen

Unten siehst du den Grundaufbau des Buches auf einer Musterseite. Und nun viel Glück und Erfolg beim Arbeiten mit den If-clauses & Co.!

MacCool

So sind die Buchseiten aufgebaut:

Eine „Leitfarbe" für jedes Kapitel

Regeln auf grünem Hintergrund

Tipps und kurzgefaßte Regeln

Übungen zum Anwenden und Vertiefen

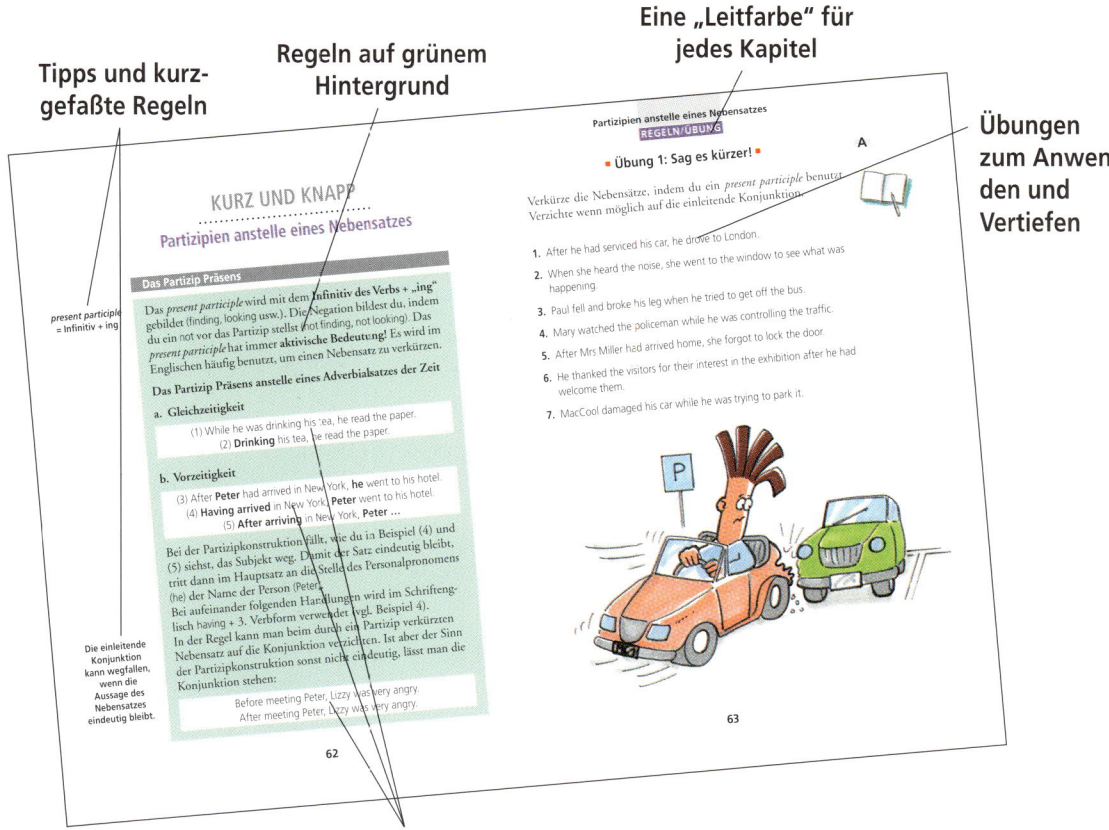

Beispielsätze

WHAT'S THAT?

Hauptsatz und Nebensatz

Begriffserklärung

Einleitung eines Nebensatzes: Konjunktion oder Relativpronomen

Bestimmt hast du die Begriffe Haupt- und Nebensatz schon im Deutschunterricht gehört. Auch im Englischen gibt es diese zwei Satzarten, wobei es einige Unterschiede in der Verwendung, Zeichensetzung und im Satzbau, aber auch viele Gemeinsamkeiten gibt. Genaueres erfährst du in den nächsten Kapiteln. Wie im Deutschen werden Nebensätze im Englischen durch Konjunktionen (when, because) oder Relativpronomen (who, which) eingeleitet.

> Peter has to learn the new words **because** he is going to have a test tomorrow.

> Peter, **who** is going to have a test tomorrow, has to learn the new words.

Nebensätze können nicht alleine stehen.

Wie im Deutschen kann der Nebensatz im Englischen nicht alleine stehen; er ist für sich alleine nicht verständlich.

> Because it is raining, …?

Findest du eine sinnvolle Ergänzung? (Lösung: Seite 84)

Wortstellung im Nebensatz

Im Unterschied zum Deutschen musst du aber nicht die Wortstellung im Nebensatz verändern. Behalte einfach die normale Wortfolge (Subjekt, Prädikat, Objekt = S P O) bei.

> We will wait here **till you have met your friend.**
> ↓ ↓ ↓ ↓ ↓
> Subjekt Prädikat Subjekt Prädikat Objekt
>
> Wir warten hier, bis du deinen Freund getroffen hast.
> ↓ ↓ ↓ ↓ ↓
> Subjekt Prädikat Subjekt Objekt Prädikat

■ Übung: Put it together! ■

MacCool hat alle Haupt- und Nebensätze durcheinander
gebracht. Kannst du sie wieder ordnen?

A

who works in a plane.

the doorbell rang.

1. Tell me about the film

after you have seen it.

6. Tim must work hard

7. Sandra always has breakfast

who looks after people, when they are ill.

you can help your mum with the dishes.

before she goes to school.

3. While Peter was doing his homework,

5. A stewardess is a woman

4. A nurse is a woman

2. When you have finished cleaning the windows,

because he is going to have a test.

1. Tell me about the film _____

2. _____

3. _____

4. _____

5. _____

6. _____

7. _____

PUNKT, PUNKT, KOMMA, STRICH ...
Die Zeichensetzung im Englischen

Hier erfährst du das Wichtigste über die Zeichensetzung im Englischen.
Der Punkt schließt immer einen Aussagesatz *(statement)* ab.

Punkt bei *statements*

> School starts at 9 in the morning.

Wie im Deutschen muss bei einer Frage *(question)* ein Fragezeichen stehen.

Fragezeichen bei *questions*

> Does school start at 9 in the morning?

Bei Ausrufen und meist auch bei Befehlen und Aufforderungen setzt du ein Ausrufezeichen ans Ende.

Ausrufezeichen bei *exclamations* und *commands*

> Oh, what a mess! Shut the window! Go away!

Im Unterschied zum Deutschen setzen die Engländer bei der wörtlichen Rede nur oben Anführungszeichen. Vor der wörtlichen Rede steht ein Komma.

Im Englischen nur Anführungszeichen (*quotation marks*) oben

> Peter said, "We are late."

Einfacher als im Deutschen ist der Gebrauch des Kommas.
1. Hauptsätze werden meist nur durch ein Komma getrennt, wenn sie nicht durch die Konjunktion "and" verbunden sind.

Vor *and* zwischen Hauptsätzen kein Komma

> Peter is watching TV and Tom is reading a book.
> Peter wasn't tired, so he watched the late movie.

2. Nebensatz und Hauptsatz werden nur durch ein Komma getrennt, wenn der Nebensatz an erster Stelle steht.

Komma, wenn der Nebensatz an erster Stelle steht

> When we were in London, wie visited the Tower.
> We went to the Tower when we visited London.

▪ Übung: Zeichensetzung ▪   A

Setze die fehlenden Satzzeichen.

1. When my husband is in Paris he'll send me a postcard

2. The visitors at the funfair were leaving when the lights went out

3. The teacher says Learn the new words

4. The door is open

5. He can't find his pen so he is writing in pencil

6. Father washed is car but he didn't polish it

7. Do you know which is the highest mountain in the world

8. Mother asks Tim Have you done your homework

9. My diamond ring is missing Somebody must have stolen it

10. I want to know if he has passed his exam

11. Does he like ice-cream

12. What a slow car this is

WANN, WO, WIE, WARUM?

Adverbialsätze

Adverbialsätze der Zeit

Adverbialsätze der Zeit drücken ein Zeitverhältnis aus. Wie im Deutschen werden sie durch Konjunktionen eingeleitet. Wenn du etwas ausdrücken möchtest, was in der **Vergangenheit** geschah, benutzt du im Englischen folgende Konjunktionen: when (als, wenn), as (während), before (bevor), since (seit), until/till (bis), after (nachdem), as soon as (sobald), while (während).

Konjunktionen wie *when*, *while* und *before* leiten Adverbialsätze der Zeit ein.

> We climbed up the Eiffel tower **when** we were in Paris.

Eine weitere Gemeinsamkeit zum Deutschen ist, dass du mit den Nebensätzen der Zeit eine Gleichzeitigkeit, Vorzeitigkeit oder einen Zukunftsbezug ausdrücken kannst.

1. Vorzeitigkeit: Hier verwendest du die Konjunktionen *after (nachdem)* und *before (bevor)*.

Adverbialsätze der Zeit können eine Vor- oder Nachzeitigkeit ausdrücken.

> **After** I had done my homework yesterday,
> I watched an interesting film.

2. Gleichzeitigkeit: Mit while (während) drückst du oft Handlungen aus, die gleichzeitig in der Vergangenheit geschehen.

> **While** Peter was working, his boss was doing nothing.

3. Zukunftsbezug: Wenn sich die Nebensätze der Zeit auf eine Handlung in der Zukunft beziehen, kannst du folgende Konjunktionen benutzen: after (nachdem), as soon as (sobald), before (bevor), by the time (wenn), until/till (bis), when (wenn).

In Nebensätzen, die sich auf die Zukunft beziehen, steht immer das *simple present*.

Achtung: Anders als im Deutschen musst du dann im Nebensatz **immer** das *simple present* benutzen.

> The Millers will move to a new flat **when** Mr. Miller
> **gets** a new job. (*nicht* will get!)

▪ Übung 1: Wann geschah's? ▪   **A**

Verbinde die Sätze mit der angegebenen Konjunktion. Setze die Kommas, falls nötig, und schreibe die Lösung in dein Heft. Vorsicht: Bei den mit !!! gekennzeichneten Sätzen musst du auch die Zeit verändern.

1. I lost a lot of weight/I was in hospital last week/while

2. Sue phoned her boy friend/
she arrived home/immediately
after!!!

3. the Vikings invaded Britain/
the Saxons fought them/
when

4. Peter will get a surprise/
he will open the door/
when!!!

5. she will get better marks/Sandra starts to work harder/as soon as

6. the Pilgrim Fathers had left Plymouth in 1620/nobody knew if they would ever reach New England/after

7. Tim's father has earned less money/he startet a new job/since

8. Grandfather was reading the newspaper/the telephone rang/while

9. they visited the Tower/they had seen the Changing of the Guard/before

10. Mandy will not be happy/she will get her exam results/until!!!

Viel einfacher als die Adverbialsätze der Zeit sind die des Ortes. Sie geben, wie der Name schon sagt, den Ort eines Geschehens an. In ihrer Verwendung gibt es keine Unterschiede zum Deutschen.

Adverbialsätze des Ortes werden durch Konjunktionen wie *where* eingeleitet.

Adverbialsätze des Ortes werden durch Konjunktionen wie where (wo), wherever (wo auch immer), somewhere (irgendwo), everywhere (überall) eingeleitet.

> The little boy follows his mother **everywhere** she goes.

Kannst du den Beispielsatz richtig übersetzen?

Der kleine _____

_____

(Lösung: Seite 84)

Beachte die unterschiedliche Zeichensetzung im Englischen und schaue noch einmal auf Seite 12 nach, wenn du dir nicht sicher bist.
Kannst du den englischen Satz nun so umstellen, dass du ein Komma setzen musst?

_____

_____

(Lösung: Seite 84)

▪ Übung 2: An Indian arrives in England ▪   A

Unterstreiche alle Adverbialsätze des Ortes.

One day an Indian arrived at Gatwick airport where crowds of people were on their way to or from London. He was carrying a heavy basket, which he put down in order to look for a luggage trolley. He couldn't find one. Wherever he looked, he could only see trolleys which were being used by other people. Suddenly he noticed a boy standing near him. The boy turned round and asked him where he came from. A man wearing dark glasses picked up the Indian's basket while he was answering the boy's question. Then the man and the boy both ran away.

The Indian looked for a policeman, but he couldn't see one anywhere, so he tried to follow the thieves.

He ran after them to the exit, where they both went into a car and drove away. He looked round the airport again: but still, wherever he looked, he could not see a policeman. He ran to a public telephone and called the police. Meanwhile, the thieves had left the town and were driving along a country road towards a wood. They stopped at a place where they felt sure that nobody could watch them. They took the basket out of the car, and tried to open it, but it was securely fastened. The man with the dark glasses fetched a screwdriver from the car. With the help of this tool he managed to open the basket.

Then the man and the boy had a big surprise. A big snake was crawling out of the basket. The Indian had been smuggling a cobra out of India.

Because, as und *since* leiten Adverbialsätze des Grundes ein.

Verwechsele nicht das kausale *since* mit dem temporalen.

Adverbialsätze des Grundes antworten auf die Fragen „Warum?" und „Wieso?". Du kannst Begründungen mit folgenden Konjunktionen einleiten:
because (weil), as (da), since (da).

> MacCool couldn't watch the late movie **because** he was too tired yesterday evening.

As und since stehen meist zu Beginn eines Satzes, because leitet häufiger Nebensätze ein, die dem Hauptsatz folgen.

> **As (Since)** MacCool hasn't learnt the new words,
> he can't write a good test.
> The children can't play outside **because** it's raining.

Pass auf! Verwechsele nicht das temporale since mit dem kausalen, das einen Grund angibt.

> **Since** it's a public holiday, your trip to England will cost a lot.
> (kausal = da)
> I have made a lot of new friends **since** we moved here.
> (temporal = seit)

Versuche beide Sätze richtig zu übersetzen:

_____

_____

_____

_____

(Lösung: Seite 85)

▪ Übung 3: Warum? ▪   B

Beantworte die folgenden Fragen auf Englisch. Achte auf die richtige Satzstellung und Zeichensetzung.

Beispiel:
Warum ist Sue heute morgen zu spät zur Schule gekommen?
(Sie musste erst zum Arzt.)
Sue came late to school this morning because she had to go to the doctor's first.

1. Warum ist Tim heute müde? (Er sah gestern den Spätfilm – late film.)

_____

_____

2. Warum spricht deine Mutter kein Englisch? (Sie hat Englisch nicht in der Schule gelernt.)

_____

_____

3. Warum verlor Borussia Dortmund das Spiel gegen Juventus Turin? (Karl-Heinz Riedle war verletzt – injured.)

_____

_____

4. Warum wurde Michael Schumacher Weltmeister (world champion)? (Er fuhr das schnellste Auto.)

_____

_____

5. Warum schrieb MacCool den besten Test? (Er hatte viel gelernt.)

_____

_____

17

Adverbialsätze des Gegensatzes

Though, although leiten Adverbialsätze des Gegensatzes ein.

Gegensätze kannst du mit folgenden Konjunktionen einleiten: although, though (obwohl), even if (auch wenn).

I'm going to buy a new car
even if I haven't got enough money yet.

Übersetze den Beispielsatz richtig:

Ich _____

_____

(Lösung: Seite 85)

Eine weitere Möglichkeit, Adverbialsätze des Gegensatzes einzuleiten, ist Konjunktionen + Adjektiv oder Adverb zu benutzen, wie z. B. however much.

Peter is going to buy the new book by Sidney Sheldon
however much it costs.

Kannst du auch diesen Beispielsatz richtig übersetzen?

_____

_____

_____

(Lösung: Seite 85)

18

▪ Übung 4: Übersetzungstraining ▪   B

Übersetze die englischen Sätze ins Deutsche und umgekehrt.

1. I'm going to go for a walk this morning even if it's raining.

_____

_____

2. Ich beabsichtige (intend) einen Computer zu kaufen, was immer er auch kostet.

_____

_____

3. However much he promises you, don't believe him.

_____

_____

4. Obwohl er heute krank ist, geht er zur Arbeit.

_____

_____

5. However expensive the new computer game is, Peter is determined to buy it.

_____

_____

6. Tina schrieb einen guten Test, obwohl sie die neuen Vokabeln nicht gelernt hatte.

_____

_____

Adverbialsätze der Art und Weise

Viele Adverbien sagen dir, auf welche Art und Weise etwas geschieht:

> Tom works quickly.
> Betty works well.

Wie arbeitet Tom? Wie arbeitet Betty?

As if (as though) und *like* leiten Adverbialsätze der Art und Weise ein.

Adverbialsätze der Art und Weise haben dieselbe Funktion. Sie werden durch die Konjunktionen as if/as though (als ob) oder like (wie, so wie) eingeleitet.

> MacCool looks **as if (as though)** he likes English grammar.
> (Wie sieht MacCool aus?)
> The actor tried to smile **like** a mad killer would smile.
> (Wie versuchte der Schauspieler zu lächeln?)

Wenn du alles mitbekommen hast, kannst du die folgenden Sätze leicht übersetzen:

> He works like slaves worked in Roman times.

_____

_____

> He works as if (as though) he enjoys it.

_____

_____

_____

Die Lösungen findest du auf Seite 85.

▪ Übung 5: Wie sieht's aus? ▪   **A**

Verbinde die passenden Satzhälften.
Achtung: Manchmal sind mehrere Lösungen denkbar, aber
eine richtige Zuordnung genügt.

1. He kissed her	**A** like Kevin Kostner fights in "Robin Hood"
2. They walked around the house	**B** as if he really loved her
3. My brother tried to fight	**C** as if they owned the place
4. The team played football	**D** like lovers do
5. Don't drive your car	**E** like teachers often do
6. He held her close	**F** like a racing driver does
7. He talked a lot	**G** like a top French chef can
8. She can cook	**H** as if they had never played before
9. They ran down the road	**I** like Boris Becker does
10. She tried to play tennis	**J** as if they were crazy

Tests: Adverbialsätze

■ Test 1: Sätze verbinden ■

Die erreichbare Punktzahl steht in Klammern.

Verbinde die beiden Sätze durch die Konjunktion in Klammern. Achte auf die richtige Zeichensetzung!

1. We had landed in Paris. We went to our Hotel. (after) (1)

_____

_____

2. The little dog follows its owner. He goes. (wherever) (1)

_____

_____

3. Sandra has caught a cold. She didn't wear a pullover. (because) (1)

_____

_____

_____

_____

4. It is hard to find work nowadays. Tim Miller has given up his old job. (though) (2)

_____

_____

5. They are going to move to a greater flat. Their baby is born. (immediately after) (2)

_____

_____

Summe (max. 7)

▪ Test 2: Was für ein Satz? ▪

Bestimme die Adverbialsätze. Kennzeichne Adverbialsätze der Zeit mit einem Z, des Ortes mit einem O, des Grundes mit GR und des Gegensatzes mit einem G.

1. While Mary was looking out of the window, she saw the bus coming. (1)

2. The fish doesn't taste good because it is too old. (1)

3. You can't make up your mind before you know the whole story. (1)

4. Although he has got a car, he's going to work by bus today. (1)

5. He will never get a good mark however hard he tries. (1)

6. Because father lost his job, we cancelled our holiday. (1)

7. After Michael Schumacher changed to Ferrari, he earned more money. (1)

8. Shall I make the tea as (because) the water is boiling now? (1)

9. While Sue was having a bath, the doorbell rang. (1)

10. Even if it's raining, Peter is going to go for a walk with his dog. (1)

Summe (max. 10)
Summe Seite 26 + 27 (max. 17)

Hast du weniger als 12 Punkte, solltest du die Seiten 12–21 noch einmal durcharbeiten!

▪ Test 3: Welche Konjunktion? ▪

Bitte setze das richtige Bindewort ein. Möglich sind **when, after, since, while, where, wherever, as if, because.**

1. _____ he had finished his homework, John watched a video. (1)

2. The policeman stopped him _____ he was driving too fast. (1)

3. I am wet and cold because the phone rang _____ I was having a bath. (2)

4. He has lived in this street _____ he moved to London from New York. (2)

5. Please tell me _____ you have finished. (1)

6. _____ I met him, he still lived in London. (1)

7. There was only a red stain left _____ the body of the murdered man had been. (1)

8. He was running for the bus _____ the devil was after him. (1)

9. He always takes his dog with him _____ he goes. (2)

10. Look at him! He is eating _____ he is really starving. (1)

Summe (max. 13)

〰〰 3 〰〰〰

IT HAD BEEN A BAD DAY for Officer Jim Chee of the Navajo Tribal Police. In fact, it had been the very worst day of an abysmal week.

It had started going bad sometime Monday. Over the week-end it had dawned upon some dimwit out at the Navajo Tribal Motor Pool that a flatbed trailer was missing. Apparently it had been missing for a considerable time. Sunday night it was reported stolen.

"How long?" Captain Largo asked at Monday afternoon's briefing, "Tommy Zah don't know how long. Nobody knows how long. Nobody seems to remember seeing it since about a month ago. It came in for maintenance. Motor pool garage fixed a bad wheel bearing. Presumably it was then parked out in the lot. But it's not in the lot now. Therefore it has to be stolen. That's because it makes Zah look less stupid to declare it stolen. Better'n admitting he just don't know what the hell they did with it. So we're supposed to find it for 'em. After whoever took it had time to haul it about as far as Florida."

Looking back on it, looking for the reason all of what followed came down on him instead of some other officer on the evening shift, Chee could see it was because he had not been looking alert. The captain had spotted it. In fact, Chee had been guilty of gazing out of the assembly room window. The globe willows that shaded the parking lot of the Shiprock subagency of the Navajo Tribal Police were full of birds that afternoon.

〰〰 28 〰〰

▪ Test 4: Übersetzungstraining ▪

Übersetze die folgenden Sätze. Achte auf die Kommasetzung!
Für jeden korrekt übersetzten Satz gibt es zwei Punkte; ist nur ein
Fehler im Satz, bekommst du immerhin noch einen Punkt.
Schreibe die Lösungen in dein Heft.

1. Wo auch immer sie suchte, Betty
   konnte ihren Hausschlüssel nicht finden.

2. Da es an der australischen Küste Haifische
   gibt, ist das Schwimmen oft verboten.

3. Als Peter das Mädchen sah, verliebte er sich sofort in sie.

4. Obwohl Herr Roberts nicht viel Geld verdient, will er sich einen Sport-
   wagen kaufen.

5. MacCool benimmt sich, als ob er noch nie ein solches Auto gesehen
   hat.

6. Linda gewinnt jedes Tennismatch, weil sie sehr viel trainiert.

7. Ich zeige dir, wo ich geboren bin.

8. Da man ihm nicht trauen kann, würde ich ihm das Geld nicht leihen.

9. John wird zum Sting-Konzert gehen, auch wenn die Karten sehr
   teuer sind.

10. Sobald Tom mit den Hausaufgaben fertig ist, wird er sich mit seinen
    Freunden treffen.

11. Während Robert das Geschirr spült, guckt Andy Fernsehen.

12. Er tanzte, wie John Travolta vor Jahren getanzt hat.

Summe (max. 24) _____
Summe Seite 24/25 (max. 37) _____

Wenn du weniger als 24 Punkte hast, solltest du das Kapitel Adverbialsätze noch einmal durcharbeiten.

ALLES RELATIV!

Relativsätze

Das Relativpronomen als Subjekt

Relativsätze sind dir bestimmt aus dem Deutschen bekannt. Hierbei handelt es sich um rückbezügliche Nebensätze, die sich auf ein Wort bzw. den ganzen vorhergehenden Hauptsatz beziehen.

> Peter, **der krank ist,** kann nicht in die Schule gehen.

Relativsätze sind rückbezügliche Nebensätze.

Relativsätze werden immer durch Relativpronomen wie der, die, das eingeleitet. Genauso verhält es sich im Englischen. Du musst also nicht viel umdenken.

> This is MacCool, **who** wants to explain relative clauses to you.

Relativpronomen: *who, which* oder *whose*

Ist das Relativpronomen, wie im Beispiel oben, das Subjekt des Relativsatzes, nimmst du bei Personen das Relativpronomen who, bei Tieren oder Sachen which. Whose (wessen/dessen) benutzt du, wenn du ein Besitzverhältnis ausdrücken willst.

> This is the bus **which** never comes on time.
> Look, this is Peter, **whose** bike has been stolen.

Tipp: Wann du beim Relativsatz im Englischen Kommas setzen musst, erfährst du auf Seite 28.

Im Unterschied zum Deutschen musst du in den englischen Relativsätzen das Relativpronomen nicht dem Numerus (Singular oder Plural) oder dem Genus (Maskulinum, Femininum, Neutrum) anpassen.

> This is the boy **who** lives in the new house.
> These are the boys **who** live in the new house.

▪ Übung 1: Sätze verbinden ▪   A

Verbinde die Sätze mit **who** oder **which.**

1. She is a secretary. She works in an office.

_____

2. There's the new magazine. It always arrives on monday.

_____

3. Over there is Peter. He is late this morning.

_____

4. This is the teacher. He teaches English.

_____

_____

5. The dog bites the postman. It's very dangerous.

_____

_____

6. The radiator is on. It has to warm up the room.

_____

7. There's Sandra. She was ill yesterday.

_____

8. The books are not worth reading. They were expensive.

_____

Vielleicht hast du dich schon gewundert, warum manche Relativsätze durch Kommas abgetrennt werden und andere nicht? Der Grund: Im Englischen unterscheidet man zwei Arten von Relativsätzen – **notwendige** und **nicht notwendige Relativsätze.**

Notwendige Relativsätze *(defining relative clauses)* erklären das Wort näher, auf das sie sich beziehen. Ohne diese Erklärung versteht man nicht, um was es geht:

> This is the boy who won the BMX race.
> The woman who stole the car was 70 years old.

Ohne den Relativsatz bleiben die Aussagen unklar (welcher Junge? welche Frau?).

Keine Kommas bei notwendigen Relativsätzen

Notwendige Relativsätze werden **nicht** durch Kommas abgetrennt.

Nicht notwendige Relativsätze *(non-defining relative clauses)* geben zusätzliche Informationen zum Wort, auf das sie sich beziehen. Sie sind zum Verständnis daher nicht unbedingt erforderlich.

Kommas bei nicht notwendigen Relativsätzen

Nicht notwendige Relativsätze werden durch Kommas abgetrennt.

> Peter, who works in a bike shop, won the BMX race.
> This is Peter, who won the BMX race.

In beiden Fällen ist auch ohne den folgenden Relativsatz klar, wer Peter ist.

▪ Übung 2: A trip to England ▪   **B**

MacCool schaut sich die Urlaubsbilder an und erklärt, was er auf den Fotos sieht.

Beispiel:
train/took us to Calais → This is the train which took us to Calais.

Welche der Relativsätze sind notwendig? Setze dort ein Komma!
Schreibe die Sätze in dein Heft.

1. ferry/took us across the Channel

2. bus/carried us to the hotel

3. guide/was very friendly and well informed

4. Linda/was ill on the ferry

5. beach/was sandy and nice

■ Übung 3: Welche Sätze gehören zusammen? ■

Welche der Relativsätze sind nicht notwendig?

1. He's my English teacher …

a. which is very dirty

2. She's the novelist …

b. whose team won the match.

3. Where are the children?

c. whose book won the first prize.

4. This is the expert …

d. who was arrested yesterday.

5. This music … sounds wonderful.

e. which was composed by Mozart.

6. This T-Shirt … belongs to MacCool.

f. whose dog is called Tim.

7. What has happened to the robber?

g. whose address I lost.

8. This is MacCool …

h. who climbed Mount Snowdon.

9. This language … is Welsh.

i. whose advice we want.

10. The Millers … spent a beautiful weekend in Wales.

j. which is difficult to understand

Verbinde die richtigen Sätze mit Pfeilen. Setze auch hier die Kommas, wenn nötig.

Das Relativpronomen als Objekt

Bis jetzt hast du das Relativpronomen nur als Subjekt des Relativsatzes oder als Besitzangabe (whose) kennen gelernt. Es kann aber genauso gut Objekt sein. Auch hier kannst du wieder Gemeinsamkeiten zur deutschen Grammatik feststellen.

> Tom ist der Mann, **den** sie liebt.

Das Relativpronomen den bezieht sich auf „Mann" und steht im Akkusativ. (Frage: Wen liebt sie?)
Im Englischen nimmst du hier die Relativpronomen who(m) oder which, je nachdem, ob du über eine Person oder eine Sache redest.

> Tom is the man **who(m)** she loves.
> Betty wrote a book **which** everybody reads.

Als Objekt ist das Relativpronomen whom zwar grammatikalisch richtig und wird auch in der Schriftsprache manchmal verwendet, es wird im alltäglichen Englisch aber meist durch who ersetzt.

Achtung: Werden die Relativpronomen in Verbindung mit Präpositionen wie in, for, to u. a. verwendet, steht bei who die Präposition am Ende des Satzes, bei whom dagegen vorne:

> He is the man **who** I wrote a letter **to.**
> He is the man **to whom** I wrote a letter.

Bei which ist beides möglich:

> The garden, **of which** Tom is very proud, is full of flowers.
> The garden, **which** Tom is very proud **of**, is full of flowers.

Wichtig: Im **notwendigen** Relativsatz kannst du das Relativpronomen weglassen, wenn es Objekt ist:

> He is the man I wrote a letter to.

Auch als Objekt nimmst du who und which in Relativsätzen.

Whom: nur im Schriftenglisch

Notwendiger Relativsatz: Wegfall des Relativpronomens als Objekt

▪ Übung 4: Auch ohne Relativpronomen ▪

Verbinde die Sätze mit **who(m)** oder **which** bzw. lasse das Relativpronomen einfach weg, wo es möglich ist.

Beispiel:
That's the cat. I photographed it.
That's the cat (which) I photographed.

1. Sue is the nurse. Tim saw her at the hospital.

   _____

   _____

2. Mrs Hill got the postcards. I sent her the postcards from Italy.

   _____

   _____

3. Mount Everest is the highest mountain. It has been climbed.

   _____

   _____

4. I have had a look at the house. We sold it ten years ago.

   _____

   _____

5. Peter often buys new toy cars. He needs them for his hobby.

   _____

   _____

6. MacCool is not the only one. He can understand this book.

   _____

▪ Übung 5: Drei Möglichkeiten ▪   A

Verbinde die Sätze auf drei verschiedene Arten.

Beispiel:
She is the woman/He sent flowers to her
a. She is the woman who he sent flowers to.
b. She is the woman to whom he sent flowers
c. She is the woman he sent flowers to.

1. Mr. Miller is the man/I sent money to him

a. _____

b. _____

c. _____

2. Over there is the building/I passed by it yesterday

a. _____

b. _____

c. _____

3. This is the shop/Peter gets all his toy cars from it

a. _____

b. _____

c. _____

4. That is the chair/I sat on it yesterday

a. _____

b. _____

c. _____

Außer bei der Kommasetzung gibt es noch einen weiteren wichtigen Unterschied zwischen **notwendigen** und **nicht notwendigen** Relativsätzen: In notwendigen Relativsätzen kannst du who, whom und which durch **that** ersetzen, in nicht notwendigen Relativsätzen geht das nicht.

Notwendige Relativsätze:

This is the boy who/**that** won the BMX race.
The woman who/**that** stole the car was 70 years old.
Did you see the book which/**that** I wanted to buy?
Yesterday Peter met the man who/**that** crossed the Atlantic Ocean.

Nicht notwendige Relativsätze:

Peter, who works in a bike shop, won the BMX race.
This is Peter, who won the BMX race.
Linda, who enjoys hiking, will spend her holidays in Switzerland.
Tom's car, which is ten years old, broke down last night.

▪ Übung 6: Who, which, that? ▪   **B**

Ersetze **who** und **which** durch **that**; aber nur dort, wo es möglich ist. Setze die Kommas und notiere die möglichen Pronomen in deinem Heft.

1. Tim's father who is on a business trip to Paris sent him a postcard.

2. The car which I want is no longer made.

3. The driver who has parked his car in front of my garage must move it away.

4. Look, there is the woman who won the dancing competition last night.

5. At the beginning of the century Wales which was the largest coal exporting area in the world produced one third of the world's coal.

6. The sport which Americans like best is baseball.

7. The Mount Everest which is the highest mountain in the world is very dangerous for people who want to climb it.

8. My sister lives in Alice Springs which is a place in Australia.

9. This is the tie which Peter wore last night.

10. MacCool who is very tired today must go back to bed.

11. Tom who I have known for ages is my best friend.

Denke an die
richtige
Kommasetzung!
Pro richtigen Satz
gibt es einen
Punkt.

Tests: Relativsätze

▪ Test 1: Relativsätze bilden ▪

Verbinde die Sätze mit dem richtigen Relativpronomen und setze
den Relativsatz an die richtige Stelle. Wo ist auch **that** möglich?

1. Did you get the letter? I sent it to you last friday.

_____

_____

2. Peter was late this morning. It had to be expected.

_____

_____

3. Tom's father found his car keys. He had lost them three days before.

_____

_____

4. The BMX bike has no lights. Sandra rides this bike to school.

_____

_____

5. We have a nice little dog. It likes to sit on the sofa.

_____

_____

6. I had a look at the ruins of the house. It was destroyed by lightning.

_____

_____

Summe (max. 6)

▪ Test 2: Wegfall des Relativpronomens ▪

Verbinde die Sätze, ohne dass du ein Relativpronomen benutzt.

1. Sue goes to school. The school is a comprehensive school.

_____

_____

2. She must wear a school uniform.
It consists of a red cap and a red blazer.

_____

_____

_____

3. That's the film star. I met him at my hotel yesterday.

_____

_____

4. Look at this book. My brother got it from his friend.

_____

_____

5. This is one of her teachers. She has him for English and Sport.

_____

_____

6. Where's the car? Tom parked it in front of my garage yesterday.

_____

_____

Summe (max. 12)

▪ Test 3: Was weißt du über Großbritannien? ▪

Auf dieser Karte von GB findest du sieben Städte. Wenn du sie kennst, schreibe auf, was du über sie weißt bzw. wo sie liegen. Benutze dabei Relativsätze.

Tipp: Die Stichwörter helfen dir bei der Antwort.

Beispiel:
Number 8 is Nottingham, which is well-known because of Robin Hood.

Northern Ireland

famous for the Beatles

the capital of England

situated on the Bristol channel

a footballteam called Glasgow Rangers

the historical capital of Scotland

well-known because of Robin Hood

well-known port

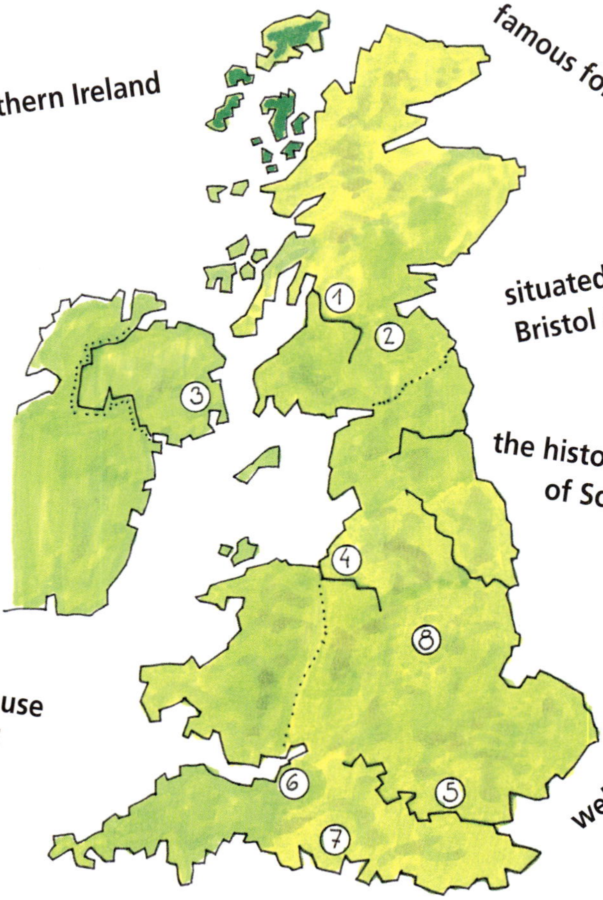

Jede richtig erkannte Stadt gibt einen Punkt. Wenn du unsicher bist, schlag in deinem Atlas nach! Du kannst in diesem Test max. 7 Punkte erreichen.

Summe:

▪ Test 4: Übersetzungstraining ▪

Für jede richtige Lösung kannst du dir 1 Punkt gutschreiben!

Kannst du die folgenden Relativsätze ins Englische übersetzen? Wo ist auch **that** möglich?

1. This is the woman … *die den Preis für das beste Video gewann.*

_____

2. Do you know the boy … *dessen Familie letztes Jahr umgezogen ist?*

_____

3. The cat … *die gerne in der Sonne liegt …* belongs to Sandra.

_____

_____

4. This is a picture of the house … *in dem ich mehr als zehn Jahre gelebt habe.*

_____

5. Henry Maske is the only German … *der Weltmeister im Boxen ist.*

_____

6. Graham is the boy … *den ich eingeladen hatte, mich in Deutschland zu besuchen.*

_____

Summe (max. 6) _____

Summe Seite 34:
Summe Seite 35:
Summe Seite 36:
Summe Seite 37:
Gesamt (max. 31):

Hast du weniger als 20 Punkte, so arbeite das Kapitel Relativsätze lieber noch einmal durch!

WAS WÄRE, WENN …?

If-clauses (Bedingungssätze)

Typ I: Erfüllbare Bedingung

Bedingungssätze kennst du natürlich aus dem Deutschen. Sie werden meist mit wenn – dann gebildet. Im Englischen heißen sie *If-* oder *conditional clauses*. Dem deutschen wenn (im Sinne von falls) entspricht in diesem Fall das englische if.

> **If** Mr Parker finishes work early, he will (can) go home.
> *Wenn (Falls) Herr Parker früh mit der Arbeit fertig ist,*
> *(dann) geht er nach Hause (kann er nach Hause gehen).*

Bedingungssätze bestehen immer aus zwei Teilen: dem If-Satz oder Nebensatz und dem *main clause*, dem Hauptsatz. Es gibt drei Typen, die die Wahrscheinlichkeit einer Bedingung ausdrücken.

Typ I:
Erfüllbare
Bedingung

Typ I drückt eine Bedingung aus, die noch geschehen kann bzw. die in der Zukunft noch erfüllbar ist. Im If-Satz steht *present tense*, im *main clause* will-*future*, can, may oder must + Infinitiv.

Typ I:
If-Satz: *present*
tense
Hauptsatz:
*will-*future, *can,*
may oder
must + Infinitiv

Ob der If-Satz an erster oder zweiter Stelle steht, hat auf die Verwendung der Zeiten keinen Einfluss. Achte dabei nur auf die richtige Zeichensetzung! (vgl. Seite 12)

> I will finish the book I'm reading if I have time tonight.
> If I have time tonight, I will finish the book …

Wichtig: Benutze nie das will-*future* im If-Satz!

Pass auf: Verwechsele nicht if (konditional) mit when (temporal) (vgl. Seite 14). Im Deutschen kannst du beides mit wenn übersetzen.

■ Übung 1: Satzpuzzle ■   A

Verbinde die If-Sätze aus der linken Spalte mit den passenden *main clauses* aus der rechten Spalte.

1. If you go by train,

2. If the sun is shining,

3. If John has time this week,

4. If you are leaving at 6 o'clock

5. If Peter stays until 7,

6. If I learn the new words,

7. If you go to London,

8. If Sandra goes by car,

9. If it is raining this afternoon,

10. If you forget to phone,

a. he'll visit us.

b. you must see the Tower of London.

c. you will be on time.

d. he will meet my best friend.

e. you won't meet my mother.

f. she will not be on time.

g. we will go for a picnic.

h. I'll get a good mark.

i. they will go without you.

j. I can't plant the vegetables.

Gar nicht so einfach …

▪ Übung 2: If, if, if … ▪

Setze die richtige Verbform ein.

1. If you _____ (see) him, you _____ (give) him this letter.

2. If it _____ (be) too hot in the room, you _____ (turn down) the heating.

3. If Peter _____ (forget) to reserve the tickets, they _____ (be not able to) to visit the football match.

4. If you _____ (ask) me nicely, I _____ (give) you the information.

5. I _____ (pay) for you if you _____ (come to) the concert with me.

6. If you _____ (not take) a taxi, you _____ (miss) the plane.

7. I _____ (try to get it done) during the week if Tom _____ (not finish) his job this week.

8. If we _____ (stay) in this flat till June, we _____ (have) problems selling it.

9. You _____ (be) in trouble if you _____ (not stop) borrowing money.

10. If he _____ (drink) too much this evening, he _____ (not go by car).

11. Sam _____ (get) a good mark in maths if he _____ (work) hard all week.

▪ Übung 3: Der Umzug nach London (1) ▪   **B**

Tina ist 18 Jahre alt. Sie überlegt, von einer kleinen Stadt in Norddeutschland nach London zu ziehen. Ihr Freund Marc lebt bereits seit 7 Monaten in London. Er gibt Tina einige Tipps.

Beispiel:
go to London/have problems finding a cheap flat
If you go to London, you will have problems finding a cheap flat.

1. can only buy things cheaply/know where the shops are

   You can _____

   _____

2. live far from your job/spend a lot on bus or train fares

   If you _____

   _____

3. can't save much money/want to have fun

   You can't _____

   _____

4. parents are worried/live alone in such a big city

   Your parents _____

   _____

5. want to make new friends/take a long time

   If you _____

   _____

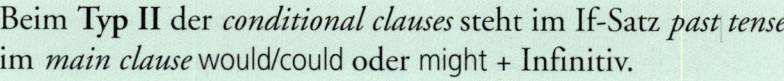

Typ II:
If-Satz: *past tense*
Hauptsatz: *would/could* + Infinitiv

Beim **Typ II** der *conditional clauses* steht im If-Satz *past tense*, im *main clause* would/could oder might + Infinitiv.

> If you **went** by train, you **would arrive** earlier.
> *Wenn du mit dem Zug fahren würdest,*
> *würdest du früher ankommen.*

Typ II:
a) Erfüllbare Bedingung
b) Nicht erfüllbare Bedingung

Typ II drückt
a. erfüllbare, aber eher unwahrscheinliche Bedingungen aus (vgl. das Beispiel oben),
b. nicht erfüllbare Bedingungen aus (vgl. das folgende Beispiel)

> If you had longer legs, you could swim faster.
> *Wenn du längere Beine hättest, könntest du schneller schwimmen.*
> *(nicht erfüllbar)*

Im Deutschen drückst du solche Bedingungen oft mit den Modalverben würde, könnte, dürfte usw. aus.

Achtung: Willst du eine nicht erfüllbare Bedingung mit dem Hilfsverb to be ausdrücken, kannst du bei allen Personen (I, you, he, she, it ...) die Form were benutzen.

> If I **were** you, I would run faster.

In der Umgangssprache wird aber auch hier **was** benutzt.

In einigen Fällen gebraucht der Engländer das Modalverb might + Infinitiv im *main clause*. Damit will er ausdrücken, dass er sich nicht sicher ist, ob ein Ereignis eintritt, selbst wenn die Bedingung dafür erfüllt ist.

> If he worked very hard, he **might** pass the exam.

Wichtig: Das *simple past* im If-Satz drückt **nicht** aus, dass die Handlung **in der Vergangenheit** geschieht!

▪ Übung 4: Der Umzug nach London (2) ▪   B

Kannst du dich noch an Tina erinnern, die nach London ziehen wollte (vgl. Seite 43)? Nachdem sie mit Marc gesprochen hat, überlegt sie, was die idealen – wenn auch nicht sehr wahrscheinlichen – Bedingungen für einen Umzug wären. Bilde If-Sätze des Typs II!

Beispiel:
win the lottery/not have problems finding a flat
If I won the lottery, I would not have problems finding a flat.

1. my father be a millionaire/can buy things I want

If my father _____

_____

2. rent a flat in the City/not have to spend a lot on bus and train fares

If I _____

_____

_____

3. can save a lot of money/not (want) (to) have fun everyday

I could _____

_____

4. Mum and Dad be not worried/live in such a big city

Mum and Dad _____

_____

5. give a big welcome party and invite a lot of nice people/not take a long time to make some new friends

If I _____

_____

▪ Übung 5: Christina's dreams ▪

Auf der linken Seite siehst du die Träume von Christina. Setze die richtige Verbform ein (Typ II).

1. If I _____ (marry) a rich man, I _____ (live) in a wonderful house. **2.** I _____ (have) a lot of cats and dogs if _____ (live) in my own house. **3.** If I _____ (want to go shopping), our chauffeur _____ (can drive) me round in our Rolls. **4.** If I _____ (buy) a new ring, I _____ (can pay) with my credit card. **5.** A cook _____ (prepare) a fine meal for us if we _____ (want) to eat at home. **6.** If I _____ (have) a swimming pool, I _____ (lie) beside it in the sun. **7.** I _____ (give) a big party for all my friends if I _____ (feel) lonely. **8.** If I _____ (have) time, I _____ (travel) all over the world. **9.** If I _____ (want) to go up the Eiffel Tower or if I _____ (want) to visit the Louvre, I _____ (hire) a private plane to Paris. **10.** If I _____ (be married) to a rich man, I _____ (make) all my dreams come true.

▪ Übung 6: Visiting London ▪

B

Auf ihrer Heimreise von London diskutiert Familie Meier die Vor- und Nachteile eines erneuten Besuches. Hier ihre Argumente dafür *(advantages)* und dagegen *(disadvantages)*.

		advantages	**disadvantages**
	Go to London again	do more shopping	spend more money.
1.	Take the train	save a lot of time	have to stay together.
2.	Visit the Tower	see the Crown Jewels	have to queue.
3.	Go to Oxford Street	find new shops	see a lot of people.
4.	Climb up St. Paul's	have a beautiful view	have to climb a lot of stairs.
5.	Take a hotel at Piccadilly Circus	be in the centre	be very noisy.

Ein Teil der Kronjuwelen

Beispiel:
If we went to London again, we could do more shopping but we would also spend more money.

1. If we took … _____

_____

2. _____

_____

St. Paul's Cathedral

3. _____

_____

4. _____

_____

5. _____

_____

Piccadilly Circus

▪ Übung 7: Typ I oder Typ II? ▪

A

Nun musst du entscheiden, um welchen Satztyp es sich handelt.
Setze die richtige Verbform ein.

1. You can always ask a policeman if you _____ (get) lost in London.

2. If Christina _____ (be) rich, she would buy a lot of new clothes.

3. He can pay the bill if he _____ (get) his cheque today.

4. If he didn't do well in his present job, he _____ (think) about getting a new one.

5. We could be more independent if we _____ (run) our own business.

6. If Susan borrowed your book, she _____ (return) it.

7. He will find a solution if he _____ (understand) the problem.

8. If I _____ (be) a millionaire, I _____ (live) in a palace.

9. If I _____ (be) you, I _____ (learn) the new grammar.

10. We will climb the Eiffel tower if we _____ (go) to Paris next year.

11. If he _____ (become) famous, he _____ (give) a lot of parties.

▪ Übung 8: Übersetzungstraining ▪ B

Übersetze die Sätze, indem du Typ I oder Typ II verwendest. Achte auf die Kommas!

1. Wenn es regnet, können wir nicht draußen spielen.

_____

_____

2. Wenn Tom Vokabeln lernen würde, könnte er einen besseren Test schreiben.

_____

_____

3. Wenn ich meinen Lehrer fragen würde, könnte er mir eine Antwort geben.

_____

_____

4. Wenn Peter mit dem Fahrrad fährt, wird er schneller sein.

_____

_____

5. Sues Familie könnte mehr Geld sparen, wenn die Wohnung billiger wäre.

_____

_____

6. Wenn du in eine andere Stadt ziehst (move), wird es lange dauern, neue Freunde zu finden.

_____

_____

B

Sandra und Martin unterhalten sich über ihre Sommerferien. Während Sandra konkrete Pläne schmiedet, will Martin eigentlich zu Hause bleiben. Bilde If-Sätze!

1. Sandra: If we go to Coventry, … (to be able to/visit/ famous cathedral).

2. Martin: Yes, but if we went there, … (cannot swim).

3. Sandra: If we drive to Eastbourne, … (can swim).

4. Martin: Yes, but if … (cannot do mountain climbing).

5. Sandra: If we travel to the Highlands, … (can do mountain climbing).

6. Martin: Yes, but if … (to be impossible to visit museums).

7. Sandra: If we take the train to London, … (can visit museums).

8. Martin: Yes, but if … (cannot do fishing).

9. Sandra: If we spend our holidays in Yorkshire, … (can do fishing).

10. Martin: Yes, but if … (cannot visit cathedral).

Sandra: All right! Let's stay at home this year.

Abbildungen links
(von oben nach unten):
Coventry; Eastbourne;
Loch Shiel (Highlands);
Trafalgar Square (London);
Yorkshire

If-clauses (Bedingungssätze)

▪ Übung 10: Hier stimmt was nicht! ▪   **A**

In jedem dieser Sätze ist ein Fehler. Finde und verbessere ihn, indem du den korrekten Satz in dein Heft schreibst.

1. You can always ask a policeman if you got lost in London.

2. I could visit the Tower of London if we had stayed for two more days.

3. There wouldn't be a statue of Lord Nelson in Trafalgar Square if he loses the battle against the French fleet.

4. You can always listen to funny people if you could go to Speakers' Corner.

5. If you want to get from Oxford Street to the Tower by Underground, you would have to take the Bakerloo line.

6. If we wanted to see Cleopatra's needle, we could have gone on a boat trip on the Thames.

7. You could visit dozens of museums in London if you had liked to.

8. If Prince Charles becomes King of England, the coronation (Krönung) would take place at the famous St. Paul's Cathedral.

9. If you miss the Changing of the Guard, you could still see it later.

10. If I am you, I would spend my next holidays in London.

11. If the weather will be fine in London, you will really love it.

Abbildungen rechts
(von oben nach unten):
Chef der Garde im Tower;
Hyde Park/Speaker's Corner;
Buckingham Palace/
Changing of the Guard

Typ III:
If-Satz:
past perfect
Hauptsatz:
would + have +
3. Form

Beim **Typ III** der *conditional clauses* steht im If-Satz das *past perfect*, im *main clause* **would/could** + **have** + 3. Form *(conditional II)*

> If we **hadn't sold** our house last year,
> we **would have lived** there up to now.

Im Deutschen musst du diesen Satz im Konjunktiv II wiedergeben, den es im Englischen nicht gibt.

> *Wenn wir unser Haus letztes Jahr*
> *nicht verkauft hätten,*
> *hätten wir bis heute dort gelebt.*

Typ III:
Unmögliche oder
nicht erfüllte
Bedingung

Du verwendest **Typ III** für Bedingungen, die sich auf die Vergangenheit beziehen. Sie sind daher in der Gegenwart nicht mehr zu erfüllen.

Wenn auch bei einer in der Vergangenheit erfüllten Bedingung die Schlussfolgerung recht unsicher ist, kannst du das Modalverb **might** + **have** + 3. Form benutzen.

> If Peter had known the facts, he **might have done** the right thing.
> *Falls Peter die Tatsachen gekannt hätte,*
> *hätte er (vielleicht) das Richtige getan.*

▪ Übung 11: Schlussfolgerungen ▪   A

Kommentiere die folgenden Sätze, indem du Bedingungssätze des dritten Typs verwendest.

Beispiel:
Mike ate too many hot dogs, so he felt sick.
If Mike hadn't eaten too many hot dogs, he wouldn't have felt sick.

1. The new school didn't burn down because the fire brigade came
immediately.

_____

_____

2. I had an accident because I didn't see the red light.

_____

_____

3. I was sweating because I was playing football for two hours.

_____

_____

4. My mother wasn't able to do the shopping because she was ill.

_____

_____

5. Sam didn't enjoy school, so he got bad marks.

_____

_____

6. Peggy fastened her seatbelt, so she wasn't hurt in the accident.

_____

_____

▪ Übung 12: Was wäre, wenn …? ▪

Eigentlich hätte alles auch anders laufen können! Bilde If-Sätze.

Beispiel:
Tom won the lottery. He bought a very expensive car.
If Tom hadn't won the lottery, he wouldn't have bought a very expensive car.

1. Tim's father had fastened his seatbelt. He was not hurt in the accident.

_____

_____

2. Sandra went for a walk with her dog in the rain. She caught a cold.

_____

_____

3. MacCool didn't learn the new grammar rules. He failed in the test.

_____

_____

4. Tom wanted to stay in London. He didn't take the well paid job in Munich.

_____

_____

5. Mary bought a new dress for £ 200,–. Her mother got angry.

_____

_____

6. John didn't like driving. He always went by train.

_____

_____

▪ Übung 13: Pauls Tag ▪   A

Gestern gingen Paul einige Dinge völlig daneben, andere Sachen gelangen jedoch. Was wäre, wenn …? Schreibe die Lösungen in dein Heft!

Beispiel:
Paul didn't hear his alarm clock, so he was not on time.
If Paul had heard his alarm clock, he would have been on time.

1. Paul's breakfast was not ready because his mother was ill.

2. His bike had a puncture, so he had to go to school by bus.

3. He arrived at school too early because he had taken the bus.

4. In the first lesson he got all answers to the test right because he had prepared for it.

5. He had no money for milk, so he didn't buy any in the break.

6. After coming home he wasn't able to do his homework because he had left his books at school.

7. He repaired his bike because he had enough time.

8. He wasn't tired, so he watched the late movie.

55

Das Wichtigste auf einen Blick!

Bevor du dich an den Abschlusstest machst, möchte MacCool mit dir noch einmal alle Regeln zu den *If-clauses* wiederholen.

Wir unterscheiden drei Typen *If-clauses:*

Typ I: Im If-Satz steht *present tense*, im *main clause* **will**-*future* oder **can/must/may** + Infinitiv.

Typ I drückt **erfüllbare Bedingungen** aus.

> If Mum **goes** by train, she **will get** there more cheaply.

Typ II: Im If-Satz steht *past tense*, im *main clause* **could/would** oder **might** + Infinitiv.

Typ II kann sowohl **erfüllbare (aber unwahrscheinliche)** als auch **nicht erfüllbare** Bedingungen ausdrücken.

> If Mum **went** by train, she **would get** there more cheaply.
> If Mum **won** a million pounds, she **would go** by private plane.

Typ III: Im If-Satz steht *past perfect*, im *main clause* **would/could** oder **might** + **have** + 3. Form.

Typ III drückt Bedingungen in der **Vergangenheit** aus (die daher in der Gegenwart **nicht mehr erfüllbar** sind).

> If Mum **had gone** by train, she **would have got** there more cheaply.

Tests: If-clauses

Setze die richtige
Verbform ein.
Pro richtiges Verb
gibt es einen
Punkt.

■ Test 1: Kontrast Typ I + II + III ■

1. If you don't lend me the money I need,

   I _____ (must go) to the bank. ____

2. I would go to university if I _____ (be) you. ____

3. If Germany _____ (not lose) the second World ____

   War, Germany _____ (not become) democratic. ____

4. Peter _____ (be able to see) the Eiffel Tower ____

   if he went to Paris.

5. Susan would have caught the school bus if she

   _____ (wake up) earlier. ____

6. If you need help in London, you _____ (ask) a policeman. ____

7. I _____ (enjoy) the party more if I _____ (not drink) too ____

   much yesterday evening.

8. If Tina has time, she _____ (see) the new James Bond film. ____

9. If you _____ (not practise) your English every day, you ____

   _____ (forget) it. ____

10. Tony would buy a more expensive bike if he _____ (save) ____

    enough money.

11. If you waited long enough at No. 10 Downing Street, you

    _____ (be able to see) the British Prime Minister. ____

12. If I _____ (be) you , I would try to do this exercise well. ____

Summe (max. 15) ____

▪ Test 2: The Indians on the war-path ▪

Forme die unterstrichenen Sätze in Bedingungssätze des dritten Typs um. Für jeden richtig umgeformten Satz gibt es in dieser Übung zwei Punkte. Schreibe die If-Sätze in dein Heft.

"We'll know hunger soon," said Red Cloud to Sitting Bull. The two Indian chiefs were looking down on the prairie. <u>Hundreds of dead buffalo were lying there.</u> <u>"The white men have killed all those animals, just for their tongues,"</u> said Sitting Bull. "We can't let them go on." The white hunters had cut the buffalo tongues out, leaving the rest. <u>Buffalo tongue was a great and expensive delicacy when sold in the butcher's shops in the Eastern States, so hundreds of hunters came to shoot the animals.</u> But the Indians needed their buffalo herds, which did not only provided them with meat. They provided them with clothes to wear and bones to burn, so that they could survive the hard winters.
<u>In 1864, when they had been building the railroad to the Pacific, the railway company had killed even more buffalo.</u> After that, the prairie itself was used as a vast game reserve, and people even came to shoot buffalo from the train windows, for sport. The Indians knew that the building of the railway and the killing of the buffalo threatened their traditional way of life. <u>At first the big steam engines made the Indians run away, so they didn't attack the railroad.</u> <u>But after they had lost their fear, they attacked the railway.</u>
Another war against the white man began. Sitting Bull won one victory over General Custer but the Indians could not stop the white settlers from taking their land. <u>The white man destroyed the Indian way of life, and since that time, many Indians have been forced to spend their lives on reservations.</u>

Beispiel:
If the white man had not killed the animals for their tongues, hundreds of dead buffalo wouldn't have been lying there.

Summe (max. 10)

TESTS

▪ Test 3: Das Dartspiel ▪

Setze die richtige Verbform ein (Typ I). Jeder richtige
Satz auf dieser Seite ergibt einen Punkt.

1. If the darts player _____ (hit) the centre, he _____
(score) 50 points.

_____

2. If he _____ (not hit) the board, he _____ (not score) any
points.

_____

3. The darts player _____ (score) 10 points if he _____ (hit)
the centre circle.

_____

4. If he _____ (want) to win, he _____ (must) score at least
25 points.

_____

5. If he _____ (not score) 25 points, he _____ (not win).

_____

Summe (max. 5) _____

▪ Test 4: *If* oder *when?* ▪

1. I'll come home _____ the meeting is over.

_____

2. Santa Claus has to do a lot _____ Christmas comes.

_____

3. _____ I lived in a bigger flat, I would have two dogs.

_____

4. We won't catch the bus _____ we don't hurry.

_____

5. I lost a lot of weight _____ I was in hospital last week.

_____

6. The robbers had escaped _____ the police arrived.

_____

7. _____ MacCool were a millionaire, he would live in an old
castle.

_____

8. You won't get seasick _____ you take a tablet.

_____

Summe (max. 8) _____

59

■ Test 5: Typ I/Typ II/Typ III ??? ■

Auch hier kannst du dir für jeden richtigen Satz
einen Punkt gutschreiben.

1. He is so mean that he _____ (not lend) you
a penny even if you gave him security for it.

2. What _____ (you say) if I told you that John
was a spy?

3. If something had gone wrong, _____ Jack _____ (know)
how to deal with the matter?

4. If you _____ (be bitten) by a snake, what would you do?

5. If King James had been wiser, he _____ (not lose) his throne.

6. If the man had committed the murder, he _____ (be hung).

7. If you had started your own library a few years ago, you _____
(have) a good collection of books by now.

8. She _____ (be) very pleased if she had got the job.

9. All this would not have happened if the parents _____ (be)
back on time.

Summe (max. 9)

▪ Test 6: Übersetzungstraining ▪

Übersetze die Bedingungssätze ins Englische und schreibe sie in dein Heft. Achte auf die richtige Zeit!

1. Wenn du die Seiten 40–56 liest, wird diese Übung ganz einfach für dich sein. (2 Punkte)

2. Wenn du noch weitere 45 Minuten warten würdest, könntest du den Wachwechsel am Buckingham-Palast sehen. (2)

3. Falls du nach New York fahren würdest, welche Sehenswürdigkeiten würdest du gerne sehen? (1)

4. Wenn das Wetter nicht so schlecht gewesen wäre, hätte ich dich gestern besucht. (2)

5. Mir hätte die Party viel mehr Spaß gemacht, wenn Sandra gekommen wäre. (2)

6. Wenn ich heute Abend nicht müde bin, gehe ich mit meinen Freunden auf eine Party. (1)

7. Wenn Boris Becker in Wimbledon nicht gewonnen hätte, wäre er nicht so bekannt geworden. (1)

Summe (max. 11)

Summe Seite 57:
Summe Seite 58:
Summe Seite 59:
Summe Seite 60:
Summe Seite 61:
Gesamt (max. 58):

Hast du weniger als 40 Punkte, wiederhole das Kapitel noch einmal!

KURZ UND KNAPP
··
Partizipien anstelle eines Nebensatzes

present participle
= Infinitiv + ing

Das *present participle* wird mit dem **Infinitiv des Verbs + „ing"** gebildet (finding, looking usw.). Die Negation bildest du, indem du ein not vor das Partizip stellst (not finding, not looking). Das *present participle* hat immer **aktivische Bedeutung!** Es wird im Englischen häufig benutzt, um einen Nebensatz zu verkürzen.

Das Partizip Präsens anstelle eines Adverbialsatzes der Zeit

a. Gleichzeitigkeit

> (1) While he was drinking his tea, he read the paper.
> (2) **Drinking** his tea, he read the paper.

b. Vorzeitigkeit

> (3) After **Peter** had arrived in New York, **he** went to his hotel.
> (4) **Having arrived** in New York, **Peter** went to his hotel.
> (5) **After arriving** in New York, **Peter** ...

Bei der Partizipkonstruktion fällt, wie du in Beispiel (4) und (5) siehst, das Subjekt weg. Damit der Satz eindeutig bleibt, tritt dann im Hauptsatz an die Stelle des Personalpronomens (he) der Name der Person (Peter).

Bei aufeinander folgenden Handlungen wird im Schriftenglisch having + 3. Verbform verwendet (vgl. Beispiel 4).

In der Regel kann man beim durch ein Partizip verkürzten Nebensatz auf die Konjunktion verzichten. Ist aber der Sinn der Partizipkonstruktion sonst nicht eindeutig, lässt man die Konjunktion stehen:

Die einleitende Konjunktion kann wegfallen, wenn die Aussage des Nebensatzes eindeutig bleibt.

> Before meeting Peter, Lizzy was very angry.
> After meeting Peter, Lizzy was very angry.

▪ Übung 1: Sag es kürzer! ▪   A

Verkürze die Nebensätze, indem du ein *present participle* benutzt. Verzichte wenn möglich auf die einleitende Konjunktion.

1. After he had serviced his car, he drove to London.

2. When she heard the noise, she went to the window to see what was happening.

3. Paul fell and broke his leg when he tried to get off the bus.

4. Mary watched the policeman while he was controlling the traffic.

5. After Mrs Miller had arrived home, she forgot to lock the door.

6. He thanked the visitors for their interest in the exhibition after he had welcome them.

7. MacCool damaged his car while he was trying to park it.

Auf der Seite 62 hast du gelernt, wie man Adverbialsätze der Zeit durch ein *present participle* verkürzen kann. Natürlich gilt dies auch für

c. Adverbialsätze des Grundes

As MacCool had never visited such a big city before, he felt rather lost.
Never having visited such a big city before, MacCool felt rather lost.

Because MacCool thought he was late, he hurried.
Thinking he was late, MacCool hurried.

Bei Nebensätzen des Grundes fällt die Konjunktion in der Partizipkonstruktion immer weg.
Ist das Hilfsverb be Prädikat des Nebensatzes, bildest und verwendest du das *present participle*, wie du es gelernt hast.

As Tom was ill last week, he wasn't able to play football.
Being ill last week, Tom wasn't able to play football.

d. Adverbialsätze des Gegensatzes

Nebensätze, die mit (al)though eingeleitet werden, kann man ebenfalls durch ein Partizip ersetzen. Die Konjunktion bleibt dann zur Verdeutlichung des Sinns stehen.

Although Lizzy had been to England several times, she had never seen the tower.
Although having been to England several times, Lizzy had never seen the tower.

Though Tom felt ill, he went to work.
Though feeling ill, Tom went to work.

■ **Übung 2: Auch hier geht's kürzer** ■   **B**

Verkürze die Nebensätze, indem du ein *present participle* verwendest.

1. As he had watched the late movie yesterday evening, MacCool went to bed early.

2. Although MacCool was wearing white jeans, he worked in the garden.

3. While George was leaning on the gate, he chatted to his friend.

4. Because Linda was new at school, she was shy.

5. Because he has won a million pounds, MacCool wants to buy a Ferrari.

6. When you are looking for a new cooker, come to our studios.

65

Das *present participle* verkürzt einen aktiven Relativsatz, in dem das **Relativpronomen Subjekt** ist (vgl. Seite 26 ff.). Das Relativpronomen wird in diesem Fall weggelassen.

> The man who is working in the bank is helpful.
> The man **working** in the bank is helpful.
>
> There's the cat which belongs to our neighbour.
> There's the cat **belonging** to our neighbour.

Möglich ist diese Form der Verkürzung vorwiegend bei **notwendigen** Relativsätzen.

So, und nun fasst MacCool noch einmal das Wichtigste für dich zusammen:

Zusammenfassung *present participle*

Das solltest du dir merken!

1. Das *present participle* wird mit dem Infinitiv + ing gebildet (looking/not looking).

2. Bei zwei aufeinander folgenden Handlungen wird die Form having + 3. Form benutzt (having written).

3. Die Konjunktion, die den Nebensatz einleitet, kann wegfallen, wenn der Sinn des Satzes eindeutig bleibt.

4. Die Konjunktion although muss immer erhalten bleiben, die Konjunktionen des Grundes (as, because, since) werden immer weggelassen.

5. Das *present participle* kann
   – Adverbialsätze der Zeit
   – Adverbialsätze des Grundes
   – Adverbialsätze des Gegensatzes
   – Relativsätze verkürzen.

Und nun viel Erfolg bei den Übungen!

▪ Übung 3: Partizip statt Relativsatz ▪   A

Ersetze den Relativsatz durch eine Partizipkonstruktion.

Beispiel:
Look at that man who is selling ice-cream.
Look at that man selling ice-cream.

1. The plane which is flying over us is not from LTU.

_____

2. The candidates who are waiting for the test are very nervous.

_____

3. The pilot who acted very carefully changed the course.

_____

4. Passengers who travel by ship should know how to use a life-jacket.

_____

5. The man who is waiting for the boss is applying for a job.

_____

6. The company which produces those cars is based in Chicago.

_____

7. The bobby who is telling Tom the right way is very friendly.

_____

▪ Übung 4: Das geht auch anders! ▪

Ersetze die unterstrichenen Satzteile
durch eine Partizipkonstruktion.

1. <u>Tourists who take their cars with them</u>
   to Great Britain have to get used to left-hand driving.

2. <u>Whenever she visited her aunt</u>, she took a home-made cake with her.

3. <u>After you have heard my side of the story</u>, you should ask John about
   it.

4. <u>Although he has not much money left</u>, he is going to buy a very
   expensive watch.

5. <u>When he tried to learn his lessons yesterday</u>, he was disturbed by his
   mother.

6. <u>After he had done his homework</u>, he watched TV.

7. <u>When Peter turns on the lights</u>, he is surprised to find his dog sleeping
   in his bed.

▪ Übung 5: Übersetzungstraining ▪

Übersetze die Sätze ins Englische, indem du das *present participle*
benutzt.

1. Züge, die diese Station verlassen, brauchen eine Stunde bis nach
   London.

2. Als sie die Nachricht hört, eilt sie zu ihrem Nachbarn.

3. Sandra bemerkte einen auffälligen (strange-looking) Mann, der das
   Restaurant betrat.

4. Nachdem er den Brief gelesen hatte, telefonierte er sofort mit seiner
   Mutter.

5. Touristen, die mit dem Flugzeug reisen, sollten nicht rauchen.

▪ Übung 6: Was passt? ▪   A

Setze die Partizipien richtig ein.

wanting   knowing   preparing   having   doing
waiting   finding   not wearing   working   arriving

1. We saw the football fans at the station _____ for a train.

2. _____ out that the driver had stolen money, the management sacked him. (rausschmeißen)

3. There are not enough jobs for students _____ to work during the holidays.

4. The headmaster is angry with some girls for _____ their school ties.

5. After _____ her housework, mother does the shopping.

6. Don't get into any arguments before _____ the facts.

7. While _____ the meal, Mr Miller noticed that he had forgotten to buy salt and pepper.

8. After _____ breakfast, Peter's mother goes to work.

9. The woman _____ in this nice little restaurant is very friendly.

10. Since _____ in New York, we have seen a lot of this big City.

Das Partizip Perfekt

past participle:
3. Form des
Verbs, immer
passivische
Bedeutung

Das *past participle* ist die 3. Form des Verbs. Beispiele: seen, taken, liked (not seen, not taken ...) Es wird genau wie das *present participle* dazu benutzt, Nebensätze zu verkürzen. Der wichtigste Unterschied zum *present participle* ist, dass das *past participle* **passivische Bedeutung** hat.

1. Das Partizip Perfekt anstelle eines Adverbialsatzes

Adverbialsätze
der Zeit

> When MacCool was told to clean the windows again, he was angry.
> (When) **Told** to clean the windows again, MacCool was angry.

Die Form having been + 3. Form wird verwendet, um auszudrücken, dass zwei Handlungen nacheinander geschehen.

> After MacCool was told to clean the windows again, he was angry.
> **Having been told** to clean the windows again,
> MacCool was angry.

Beim Verkürzen eines Adverbialsatzes durch ein *past participle* kannst du, wenn die Aussage des Satzes eindeutig bleibt, die einleitende Konjunktion weglassen (vgl. Seite 62).

Adverbialsätze
des Grundes

> As the house had been built years ago, it wasn't in good condition.
> **Built** years ago, the house wasn't in good condition.

If-clauses

> If MacCool was told to learn the new grammar rules, he would do it.
> **If told** to learn the new grammar rules, MacCool would do it.

2. Das Partizip Perfekt anstelle eines Relativsatzes

> The furniture which is sold in this shop is the cheapest in town.
> The furniture **sold** in this shop is the cheapest in town.

▪ Übung 7: *past participle* statt Nebensatz ▪   A

Verkürze die Nebensätze mit einem *past participle*. Verzichte auf die Konjunktion, wenn der Sinn des Satzes erhalten bleibt.

Beispiel:
If the robber had been watched by the police, he would not have got very far.
If watched by the police, the robber would not have got far.

1. After Helen had been questioned by the police, she left the police station.

_____

_____

2. When he was told that there would be no test, MacCool was no longer interested in learning participle constructions.

_____

_____

3. Last week I read a book which was written by Karl May.

_____

_____

*Karl May
(1842–1912)*

4. As Sandra had been scolded (ausgeschimpft) by her mother one hour ago, she felt very sad.

_____

_____

5. If Mr Miller is fired, he will try to find a better job.

_____

6. The TV set which had been bought last week was out of order yesterday.

_____

B  ▪ Übung 8: Mayor's Son Free! ▪

Benutze für die unterstrichenen Satzteile das *past participle*. Schreibe die Lösungen in dein Heft.

Sam Owen, the boy who was kidnapped from a kindergarten in Nottingham three weeks ago, is free again. A police patrol found him in a lonely cottage two hours after the 100.000 pound ransom *(Lösegeld)*, which had been paid by his father, the mayor of Nottingham, was given to the kidnappers.

The money, which had been left at a restaurant near the motorway, was in a small suitcase. After a while three men in a sports car stopped at the place where the money had been deposited. One of the men got out, took the suitcase and put it into the car.

But the police, who were watching the men all the time, followed the car. A chase involving police cars and helicopters began as soon as the news came that Sam Owen was free and safe in Nottingham. It looked like a scene from a James Bond film.

The kidnappers' car, which was finally overtaken by the police, was ordered to stop. It drove off the road into a field, overturned and burst into flames. One kidnapper, who was thrown out of the car, tried to escape. He opened fire on the police and injured one policeman. However, he was overpowered by two other policemen. The second kidnapper, who was injured by the police, died later on. The third escaped without the money, which was left in the car. The car burnt out with all the money in it.

Later the boy's father, Mr Tom Owen, who was interviewed at his office in Nottingham by the press, said, "My son is worth more to me than 100.000 pounds. Who knows what might have happened if I had not paid the money which was demanded by the gangsters?"

Beispiel:
Sam Owen, the boy kidnapped from a kindergarten …

▪ Übung 9: Umformulieren ▪   B

Schreibe die Sätze neu, indem du die Sätze in den Klammern in *past participle*-Konstruktionen verwandelst.

Beispiel:
The child was taken to hospital. (it was injured in the accident)
The child injured in the accident was taken to hospital.

1. All people will come to the party. (the people who have been invited)

2. All letters should be sent out tomorrow. (they were written today)

3. Yesterday I discovered a book. (it was written by my grandmother)

4. The car has now been repaired. (it was brought to the garage last monday)

5. Sandra eats a cake. (it was made by her mother)

6. The Titanic tried to cross the Atlantic Ocean faster than any ship before. (it was built in 1911)

7. Martin Luther King was one of the most famous men who was fighting for the civil rights in America. (he was murdered in 1968)

8. Robert Burnes is the Scottish national poet. (he was born in Scotland)

Martin Luther King
(1929–1968)

Tests: Partizipien

■ Test 1: Contrast of *present participle* & *past participle* ■

Im folgenden Text sollst du nun entscheiden, ob du das *present* oder *past participle* verwenden musst.

Hier ein kleiner Tipp von MacCool:
Das *past participle* hat immer passivische Bedeutung! Also übersetze zuerst den Nebensatz. Stellst du fest, dass du eine Passivform (wie z. B. wird geschlagen) für die Übersetzung benötigst, nimmst du das *past participle*.
Notiere die Lösung in deinem Heft.

1. Yesterday Sam discovered a novel which had been written by his grandfather.

2. My family moved to a house which was built in the 16th century.

3. Last night a policeman who was investigating a robbery was shot.

4. The student who gets the highest marks will get a special prize.

5. The police car which followed the kidnappers hit an ambulance.

6. Tourists from outside Europe who want to visit Great Britain must join a special queue at the passport control.

7. The robber who was caught by the police last night is a well-known member of the Crane Gang.

8. Look, there are some children who are running across the street without looking left or right.

9. Because he is not perfect, MacCool makes mistakes too.

Summe (max. 9)

▪ Test 2: Welches Partizip? ▪

Setze die richtige Form des *present* oder *past participle* in die Lücken.
Für jede richtige Lösung erhältst du wieder einen Punkt!

1. _____ (sit) on the table, John talked to his friends. _____

2. After _____ (write) down his friend's telephone number, MacCool left his friend. _____

3. The girl _____ (live) next door is called Helen. _____

4. Although _____ (help) by his teacher, the pupil couldn't do the exercise. _____

5. The speaker informed the audience about homeless people _____ (need) our help. _____

6. Suddenly the pilot saw the plane _____ (fly) towards him. _____

7. Pictures _____ (take) of the celebration yesterday are published in the local newspaper today. _____

8. _____ (lose) her purse, the old woman went to the next police station. _____

9. Do you like books _____ (write) by Patricia Highsmith? _____

10. If _____ (not build) near the cliffs, the house doesn't have to be evacuated. _____

11. The students _____ (wait) for their teacher started to become noisy. _____

12. The tree _____ (stand) in our garden was cut down yesterday. _____

Summe (max. 12) _____

Summe Seite 74:
Summe Seite 75:
Gesamt (max. 21):

Wenn du weniger als 15 Punkte hast, wiederhole das Kapitel Partizipien noch einmal!

FRAGEN ÜBER FRAGEN

·······································
Abschlusstests

Nun wollen wir sehen, ob du wirklich fit bist. Wir wiederholen in diesen Abschlusstests noch einmal alles Wichtige.

■ Test I: Kannst du die Fragen beantworten? ■

1. Woran erkennst du im Englischen einen Nebensatz? (1 Punkt)

2. Kennst du die Wortstellung in einem englischen Nebensatz? (1)

3. Welche Zeitverhältnisse kannst du mit Adverbialsätzen der Zeit ausdrücken? (2)

4. Wann wird ein Nebensatz durch ein Komma vom Hauptsatz getrennt? (1)

5. Nenne vier Konjunktionen, die einen Adverbialsatz des Ortes einleiten können. (1)

6. Die Konjunktion "since" hat zwei Bedeutungen. Kennst du sie? (2)

7. Kennst du die Relativpronomen im Englischen? (1)

8. Wo steht der Relativsatz in einem Satzgefüge? (1)

Summe (max. 10)

▪ Test II: Was wäre, wenn …? ▪

Benutze If-Sätze Typ II.

Pro richtigen Satz gibt es einen Punkt!

Beispiel:
If there were no ponds, there would'nt be any frogs.

1. no frogs, no storks

_____

2. no storks, no babies

_____

3. no babies, no Germans

_____

Setze die richtige Verbform ein.

4. If my father works hard, he _____ (make) a lot of money.

5. Tony would be able to come to the next town if there _____ (be) a bus.

6. If MacCool had spoken English well last year, he _____ (visit) the USA.

7. If Tim _____ (look) at his watch yesterday, he _____ (not be) late.

8. If there's a general strike, all workers _____ (stay) at home.

9. I would try to find a hotel somewhere else if this hotel _____ (be) fully booked.

10. If this exercise is too difficult, you _____ (read) chapter five in this book.

Summe (max. 10)

▪ Test III: Television in Britain ▪

Unterstreiche alle Nebensätze in dem Text. Achtung: Manche Nebensätze sind verkürzt, wie du es vorne gelernt hast.

The British television service started in 1936 but it was closed down three years later when war broke out. It was not reopened until 1946. Television did not become a mass medium overnight. With a pre-war audience of about 20.000 homes in the London area, the service slowly extended to about 1.500.000 in 1952, covering England and Scotland. The Coronation of Queen Elizabeth II in 1953 increased the number of viewers considerably. About one million TV sets were bought in that year because many people wanted to see the broadcast of the ceremony, which was shown all over the world. In 1958 a second channel called Independent Television (ITV) was introduced. It was financed by advertising, while the BBC continued to be paid for by the licence fees which were collected from all owners of TV sets.

The new channel was so successful that from that time on the number of sets increased by about a million every year. If the new channel had not been introduced, British television would not have been so popular and successful. In the early 60s the BBC started another channel, BBC 2, and a greater variety of programmes were produced. Experiments with colour had been going on since the

birth of television. In 1953 a satisfactory system which was developed in the USA was adopted in the USA and Japan. Willy Brandt gave a speech to open the first programme shown in colour in Germany.

Other countries adopted other systems, mainly the German PAL and the French SECAM system. Nowadays every household has a colour TV set. If the TV had not been invented, a lot of people would not have known what to do in their free time.

Für jeden richtig gefundenen Nebensatz kannst du deinem Punktekonto einen weiteren Punkt gutschreiben.
Ein kleiner Tipp: 11 Nebensätze kannst du in diesem Text finden.

Punktekonto: Summe Seite 78/79 (max. 11):

Summe Seite 76/77 (max. 20):

Zwischenstand (max. 31):

▪ Test IV: Relativsätze ▪

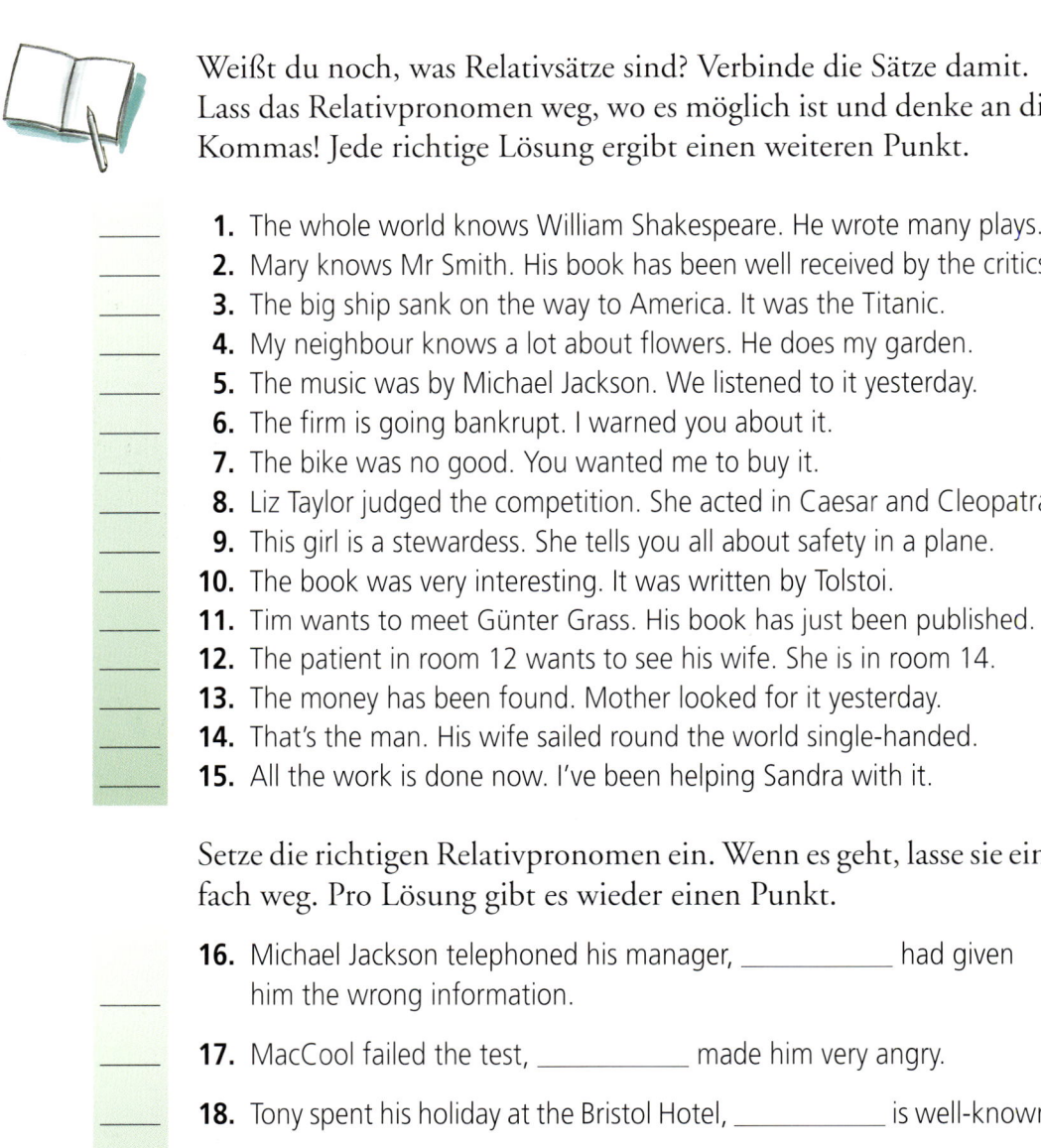

Weißt du noch, was Relativsätze sind? Verbinde die Sätze damit. Lass das Relativpronomen weg, wo es möglich ist und denke an die Kommas! Jede richtige Lösung ergibt einen weiteren Punkt.

1. The whole world knows William Shakespeare. He wrote many plays.
2. Mary knows Mr Smith. His book has been well received by the critics.
3. The big ship sank on the way to America. It was the Titanic.
4. My neighbour knows a lot about flowers. He does my garden.
5. The music was by Michael Jackson. We listened to it yesterday.
6. The firm is going bankrupt. I warned you about it.
7. The bike was no good. You wanted me to buy it.
8. Liz Taylor judged the competition. She acted in Caesar and Cleopatra.
9. This girl is a stewardess. She tells you all about safety in a plane.
10. The book was very interesting. It was written by Tolstoi.
11. Tim wants to meet Günter Grass. His book has just been published.
12. The patient in room 12 wants to see his wife. She is in room 14.
13. The money has been found. Mother looked for it yesterday.
14. That's the man. His wife sailed round the world single-handed.
15. All the work is done now. I've been helping Sandra with it.

Setze die richtigen Relativpronomen ein. Wenn es geht, lasse sie einfach weg. Pro Lösung gibt es wieder einen Punkt.

16. Michael Jackson telephoned his manager, _____ had given him the wrong information.

17. MacCool failed the test, _____ made him very angry.

18. Tony spent his holiday at the Bristol Hotel, _____ is well-known.

19. The man _____ car John crashed into is in hospital now.

20. Claudia Schiffer is a model _____ works for Karl Lagerfeld.

21. The house _____ Tim wanted to buy is very expensive.

Summe (max. 21)

■ Test V: Adverbialsätze ■

Kennst du noch alle Adverbialsätze? Unterstreiche die Nebensätze und trage die Nummer des Satzes richtig in die Tabelle unten auf der Seite ein.

1. After MacCool had come home yesterday, he did the dishes.
2. While grandfather was reading the newspaper, the telephone rang.
3. As MacCool had lost all his money, he wasn't able to pay the bill.
4. Tim follows MacCool everywhere he goes.
5. Since the weather is bad, the children can't play outside.
6. MacCool is going to buy a new BMX bike however much it costs.
7. He plays football like Pelé used to play.
8. The girl married the man although she didn't love him.
9. Because I haven't got any money, I can't go on holiday this year.
10. Sam must run to school because he has overslept this morning.
11. Although he overslept, he arrived on time.
12. Wherever he went, MacCool took his book with him.
13. After Frank Busemann had won a silver medal in Atlanta, he was welcomed home in Recklinghausen.
14. The police followed the robber everywhere he went.
15. MacCool behaves as if he doesn't speak English.

Adverbialsatz der Zeit: _____

Adverbialsatz des Ortes: _____

Adverbialsatz des Grundes: _____

Adverbialsatz des Gegensatzes: _____

Adverbialsatz der Art und Weise: _____

Jeder richtig unterstrichene und eingetragene Satz ergibt einen Punkt. Du kannst also maximal 15 Punkte in dieser Disziplin erringen.

Punktekonto:

Summe Seite 80/81 (max. 36):

Summe Seite 76–79 (max. 31):

Zwischenstand (max. 67):

■ Test VI: The Pilgrim Fathers ■

Setze ein *present* oder *past participle* ein. Für jede richtige Lösung gibt es einen Punkt!

_____ In 1608 a small group of people, _____ (want) to escape from persecution by the Church of England, left England and went to Holland. These people, who did not accept the teaching of the Church of England, considered that only they believed in the true Christ. The group
_____ _____ (want) to start a new life in Holland was able to practise their religion freely there for a number of years.

They were not happy there and they asked themselves if there might be a better life for them somewhere else. After _____ (listen) to stories
_____ told by other people about the new country on the other side of the Atlantic Ocean, some members of the community suggested making a new start in America. So the Pilgrims decided to sail to the New World.
_____ They sailed from Southampton on ships _____ (build) of wood and
_____ _____ (call) the "Speedwell" and the "Mayflower". 300 seamiles
_____ into the Atlantic the Captain of the Speedwell _____ (discover) that the ship was leaking, ordered that both ships should sail back to Plymouth.

On September 16th, 1620, a hundred and two Pilgrims finally sailed from Plymouth on the Mayflower on their 65-day journey to America. The
_____ Pilgrims, _____ (expect) to land in Virgina, were very surprised when they landed 200 miles further north on the famous Plymouth Rock near Cape Cod (later called Massachusetts). The first winter in America was terrible. The Pilgrims set up camp near the coast, but more than half
_____ the people _____ (live) in the settlement died of hunger and illness
_____ during the first winter. But later on the Pilgrims, _____ (help) by
_____ the Indians, managed to stay alive. Americans _____ (celebrate) Thanksgiving day in November each year remember the Pilgrim's first successful harvest and the feast they shared with the Indians who had helped them.

_____ **Summe (max. 10)**

*Die „Mayflower"
(Stahlstich von
John Marshall
d. Ä., um 1850)*

Punktekonto:

Summe Seite 76–81 (max. 67):

Summe Seite 82 (max. 10):

Endsumme (max. 77):

Hast du weniger als 50 Punkte in diesem Schlusstest, solltest du die Kapitel, in denen du die meisten Schwierigkeiten hattest, noch einmal wiederholen!

LÖSUNGEN

Hauptsatz und Nebensatz

Seite 8
Zum Beispiel: Because it is raining, the children can't play outside.
oder Because it is raining, Peter can't go swimming.

Seite 9
Übung 1: 1. Tell me about the film after you have seen it. 2. When you have finished cleaning the windows, you can help your mum with the dishes. 3. While Peter was doing his homework, the doorbell rang. 4. A nurse is a woman who looks after people, when they are ill. 5. A stewardess is a woman who works in a plane. 6. Tim must work hard because he is going to have a test. 7. Sandra always has breakfast before she goes to school.

Die Zeichensetzung

Seite 11
Übung 1: 1. When my husband is in Paris, he'll send me a postcard. 2. The visitors at the funfair were leaving when the lights went out. 3. The teacher says, "Learn the new words." 4. The door is open! (oder .) 5. He can't find his pen, so he is writing in pencil. 6. Father washed is car but he didn't polish it. 7. Do you know which is the highest mountain in the world? 8. Mother asks Tim, "Have you done your homework?" 9. My diamond ring is missing! (oder .) Somebody must have stolen it. 10. I want to know if he has passed his exam. 11. Does he like ice-cream? 12. What a slow car this is!

Adverbialsätze

Seite 13
Übung 1: 1. I lost a lot of weight while I was in hospital last week. 2. Sue phoned her boy friend immediately after she had arrived home. 3. When the Vikings invaded Britain, the Saxons fought them. 4. Peter will get a surprise when he opens the door. 5. As soon as Sandra starts to work harder, she will get better marks. 6. After the Pilgrim Fathers had left Plymouth in 1620, nobody knew if they would ever reach New England. 7. Tim's father has earned less money since he started a new job. 8. While Grandfather was reading the newspaper, the telephone rang. 9. Before they visited the Tower, they had seen the Changing of the Guard. 10. Mandy will not be happy until she gets her exam results.

Seite 14
Der kleine Junge folgt seiner Mutter überall, wo sie hingeht.
Everywhere his mother goes, the little boy follows her.

Seite 15
Übung 2: One day an Indian arrived at Gatwick airport where crowds of people were on their way to or from London. He was carrying a heavy basket, which he put down in order to look for a luggage trolley. He couldn't find one. Wherever he looked, he could only see trolleys which were being used by other people. Suddenly he noticed a boy standing near him. The boy turned round and asked him where he came from. A man wearing dark glasses picked up the Indian's basket while he

was answering the boy's question. Then the man and the boy both ran away.

The Indian looked for a policeman, but he couldn't see one anywhere, so he tried to follow the thieves.

He ran after them to the exit, <u>where they both went into a car and drove away.</u> He looked round the airport again: but still, <u>wherever he looked</u>, he could not see a policeman. He ran to a public telephone and called the police. Meanwhile, the thieves had left the town and were driving along a country road towards a wood. They stopped at a place <u>where they felt sure that nobody could watch them.</u> They took the basket out of the car, and tried to open it, but it was securely fastened. The man with the dark glasses fetched a screwdriver from the car. With the help of this tool he managed to open the basket.

Then the man and the boy had a big surprise. A big snake was crawling out of the basket. The Indian had been smuggling a cobra out of India. *(Falls du "where he came from" im ersten Absatz unterstrichen hast: Dies ist eine indirekte Frage, kein Adverbialsatz!)*

Seite 16
Da große Ferien sind, wird dich deine Reise nach England eine Menge kosten.
Ich habe eine Menge neuer Freunde gefunden, seit wir hierhin gezogen sind.

Seite 17
Übung 3: 1. Tim is tired today because he watched the late film yesterday. 2. My mother doesn't speak English because she didn't learn it at school. 3. Borussia Dortmund lost their match against Juventus Turin because Karl-Heinz Riedle was injured. 4. Michael Schumacher became world champion because he drove the fastest car. 5. MacCool wrote the best test because he had learned a lot.

Seite 18
Ich werde ein neues Auto kaufen, auch wenn ich noch nicht genug Geld habe.
Peter wird das neue Buch von Sidney Sheldon kaufen, was auch immer es kostet.

Seite 19
Übung 4: 1. Ich werde heute morgen spazieren gehen, auch wenn es regnet. 2. I intend to buy a new computer however much it costs. 3. Wieviel (Was auch immer) er dir auch verspricht, glaube ihm nicht. 4. Although he is ill today, he is going to work. 5. Wie teuer das neue Computerspiel auch ist, Peter ist entschlossen, es zu kaufen. 6. Tina wrote a good test although she hadn't learned the new words (new vocabulary).

Seite 20
Er arbeitet so, wie die Sklaven zur Zeit der Römer arbeiteten. Er arbeitet, als ob es ihm Spaß macht.

Seite 21
Übung 5: 1. B/1.D, 2.C, 3.A, 4.H, 5.F, 6. B/6.D, 7.E, 8.G, 9.J, 10.I

Seite 22
Test 1: 1. After we had landed in Paris, we went to our hotel. 2. The little dog follows its owner wherever he goes. 3. Sandra has caught a cold because she didn't wear a pullover. 4. Though it's hard to find work nowadays, Tim Miller has given up his old job. 5. They are going to move to a greater flat immediately after their baby is born.

Seite 23
Test 2: 1. Adverbialsatz der Zeit (Z), 2. Adverbialsatz des Grundes (Gr), 3. Adverbialsatz der Zeit (Z), 4. Adverbialsatz des Gegensatzes (G), 5. Adverbialsatz des Gegensatzes (G),

6. Adverbialsatz des Grundes (Gr), 7. Adverbialsatz der Zeit (Z), 8. Adverbialsatz des Grundes (Gr), 9. Adverbialsatz der Zeit (Z), 10. Adverbialsatz des Gegensatzes (G)

Seite 24

Test 3: 1. after (when), 2. because, 3. while, 4. since, 5. when, 6. when, 7. where, 8. as if, 9. wherever, 10. as if

Seite 25

Test 4: 1. Wherever she looked for them, Betty couldn't find her keys. 2. As (since) there are sharks on the Australian coast, swimming is often forbidden. 3. When Peter saw the girl, he fell in love at once. 4. Although (Though) he doesn't earn a lot of money, Mr Roberts wants to buy a sports car. 5. MacCool behaves as if he has never seen such a car. 6. Linda wins every (each) tennis match because she practises a lot. 7. I'll show you where I was born. 8. As (Since) you can't trust him, I wouldn't lend him the money. 9. John will go to the Sting concert even if the tickets are very expensive. 10. As soon as Tom has finished his homework, he will meet his friends. 11. While Robert is doing the dishes, Andy is watching TV. 12. He danced like John Travolta danced years ago.

Seite 27

Übung 1: 1. She is a secretary, who works in an office. 2. There's the new magazine which always arrives on monday. 3. Over there is Peter who is late this morning. 4. This is the teacher who teaches English. 5. The dog, which is very dangerous, bites the postman. 6. The radiator which has to warm up the room is on.
7. There's Sandra, who was ill yesterday. 8. The books which were very expensive are not worth reading.

Seite 29

Übung 2: 1. This is the ferry which took us across the Channel. 2. This is the bus which carried us to our hotel. 3. This is the guide, who was very friendly and well informed.
4. This is Linda, who was ill on the ferry.
5. This is the beach, which was sandy and nice. *(3., 4. und 5. sind nicht notwendige Relativsätze – sie geben Zusatzinformationen zum Reiseführer, zu Linda und zum Strand.)*

Seite 30

Übung 3: 1g. He's my English teacher, whose address I lost. 2c. She's the novelist whose book won the first prize. 3b. Where are the children whose team won the match? 4i. This is the expert whose advice we want. 5e. This music, which was composed by Mozart, sounds wonderful. 6a. This T-Shirt, which is very dirty, belongs to MacCool. 7d. What has happened to the robber who was arrested yesterday? 8f. This is MacCool, whose dog is called Tim. 9j. This language, which is Welsh, is difficult to understand. 10h. The Millers, who climbed Mount Snowdon, spent a beautiful weekend in Wales.

Seite 32

Übung 4: Sue is the nurse (who[m]) Tim saw at the hospital. 2. Mrs Hill got the postcards (which) I sent her from Italy. 3. Mount Everest is the highest mountain which has been climbed. *(Relativpronomen = Subjekt)* 4. I have had a look at the house (which) we sold ten years ago. 5. Peter often buys new toy cars (which) he needs for his hobby. 6. MacCool is not the only one who can understand this book. *(Relativpronomen = Subjekt)*

Seite 33

Übung 5: 1.a. Mr Miller is the man to whom I sent money. b. … the man who I sent money to. c. … the man I sent money to. 2. a. Over there is the building by which I passed yesterday. b. … the building which I passed by yesterday. c. … the building I passed by yesterday. 3. a. This is the shop from which Peter gets all his toy cars. b. … the shop which Peter gets all his toy cars from. c. … the shop Peter gets all his toy cars from. 4. a. That is the chair on which I sat yesterday. b. … the chair which I sat on yesterday. c. … the chair I sat on yesterday.

Seite 35

Übung 6: Tim's father, who is on a business trip to Paris, sent him a postcard. 2. The car which/that I want is no longer made. 3. The driver who/that has parked his car in front of my garage must move it away. 4. Look, there is the woman who/that won the dancing competition last night. 5. At the beginning of the century Wales, which was the largest coal exporting area in the world, produced one third of the world's coal. 6. The sport which/that Americans like best is baseball. 7. The Mount Everest, which is the highest mountain in the world, is very dangerous for people who/that want to climb it. 8. My sister lives in Alice Springs, which is a place in Australia. 9. This is the tie which/that Peter wore last night. 10. MacCool, who is very tired today, must go back to bed. 11. Tom, who I have known for ages, is my best friend.

Seite 36

Test 1: 1. Did you get the letter which/that I sent to you last friday? 2. Peter was late this morning, which had to be expected. 3. Tom's father found his car keys, which he had lost three days before. 4. The BMX bike which/that Sandra rides to school has no lights. 5. We have a nice little dog, which likes to sit on the sofa. 6. I had a look at the ruins of the house which/that was destroyed by lightning.

Seite 37

Test 2: 1. The school Sue goes to is a comprehensive school. 2. The school uniform she must wear consists of a red cap and a red blazer. 3. That's the film star I met at my hotel yesterday. 4. Look at this book my brother got from his friend. 5. This is the teacher she has for English and Sport. 6. Where's the car Tom parked in front of my garage yesterday?

Seite 38

Test 3: Number 1 is Glasgow, which has got a football team called Glasgow Rangers. / Number 2 is Edinburgh, which is the historical capital of Scotland. / Number 3 is Belfast, which is in Northern Ireland. / Number 4 is Liverpool, which is famous for the Beatles. / Number 5 is London, which is the capital of England. / Number 6 is Bristol which is situated on the Bristol channel. / Number 7 is Southampton, which is a well-known port.

Seite 39

Test 4: 1. This is the woman who (that) won the prize for the best video. 2. Do you know the boy whose family moved last year? 3. The cat which (that) likes to lie in the sun belongs to Sandra. 4. This is a picture of the house in which I have lived for more than ten years (which I have been living in …). 5. Henry Maske is the only German who (that) has (ever) become world champion in boxing. 6. Graham is the boy (who[m]) (that) I had invited to visit me in Germany.

If-clauses

Seite 41

Übung 1: 1. c., 2. g., 3. a., 4. e., 5. d., 6. h., 7. b., 8. f., 9. j., 10. i.

Seite 42

Übung 2: 1. see; can/must give, 2. is; can/must turn down, 3. forgets; will not (won't) be able to, 4. ask; will give, 5. can/will pay; come to, 6. don't take; will miss, 7. can/will try to get it done; doesn't finish, 8. stay; will have, 9. will be; don't stop, 10. drinks; can't/mustn't/won't go by car, 11. will/can/may get; works

Seite 43

Übung 3: 1. You can only buy things cheaply if you know where the shops are. 2. If you live far from your job, you must (will) spend a lot on bus or train fares. 3. You can't save much money if you want to have fun. 4. Your parents will be worried if you live alone in such a big city. 5. If you want to make new friends, it will take a long time.

Seite 45

Übung 4: 1. If my father were (was) a millionaire, I could buy things I want. 2. If I rented a flat in the city, I would not have to spend a lot on bus and train fares. 3. I could save a lot of money if I didn't want to have fun everyday. 4. Mum and Dad wouldn't be worried if I lived in such a big city. 5. If I gave a big welcome party and invited a lot of nice people, it wouldn't take a long time to find some new friends.

Seite 46

Übung 5: 1. married; would live, 2. would/could have; lived, 3. wanted to go shopping; could drive, 4. bought; could pay, 5. would prepare; wanted, 6. had; would/could lie, 7. would give; felt, 8. had; could/would travel, 9. wanted; wanted; would/could hire, 10. was (were) married; could/would make

Seite 47

Übung 6: 1. If we took the train, we could save a lot of money but we would also have to stay together. 2. If we visited the Tower, we could see the Crown Jewels but we would also

have to queue. 3. If we went to Oxford Street, we could find new shops but we would also see a lot of people. 4. If we climbed up St. Paul's, we would have a beautiful view but we would also have to climb a lot of stairs. 5. If we took a hotel at Piccadilly Circus, we would be in the centre but it would also be very noisy.

Seite 48

Übung 7: 1. get, 2. was (were), 3. gets, 4. would / could think, 5. ran, 6. would return, 7. understands, 8. was (were); would live, 9. was (were); would learn, 10. go, 11. became; would give

Seite 49

Übung 8: 1. If it rains, we can't play outside. 2. If Tom learned the words, he could write a better test (do better in the test). 3. If I asked my teacher, he could give me an answer. 4. If Peter goes by bike, he will be faster. 5. Sue's family could save more money if the flat was (were) cheaper. 6. If you move to another town, it will take a long time to find new friends.

Seite 50

Übung 9: 1. …, we will be able to visit a famous cathedral. 2. …, we couldn't swim. 3. …, we can swim. 4. … if we drove to Eastbourne, we could not do mountain climbing. 5. …, we can do mountain climbing. 6. … if we travelled to the Highlands, it would be impossible to visit museums. 7. …, we can visit museums. 8. … if we took the train to London, we could not do fishing. 9. …, we can do fishing. 10. … if we spent our holidays in Yorkshire, we couldn't visit a cathedral.

Seite 51

Übung 10: 1. if you **get** lost, 2. if we **stayed**, 3. if he **had lost**, 4. if you **go** to, 5. you **must** take *oder* **will have** to take, 6. we **could go**, 7. if you **liked** to, 8. **will take** place (oder: If Prince Charles **became**), 9. you **can** still see (oder: If you **missed**), 10. If I **were** (was) you, 11. **is** fine

Seite 53

Übung 11: 1. The new school would have burned down if the fire brigade hadn't come immediately. 2. If I had seen the red light, I wouldn't have had an accident. 3. If I hadn't been playing football for two hours, I wouldn't have been sweating. 4. If my mother hadn't been ill, she would have been able to do the shopping. 5. If Sam had enjoyed school, he wouldn't have got bad marks. 6. If Peggy hadn't fastened her seatbelt, she would have been hurt in the accident.

Seite 54

Übung 12: 1. If Tim's father hadn't fastened his seatbelt, he would have been hurt in the accident. 2. If Sandra hadn't gone for a walk with her dog in the rain, she wouldn't have caught a cold. 3. If MacCool had learned the new grammar rules, he wouldn't have failed in the test. 4. If Tom hadn't wanted to stay in London, he would have taken the well paid job in Munich. 5. If Mary hadn't bought a new dress for £ 200,–, her mother wouldn't have got angry. 6. If John had liked driving, he wouldn't always have gone by train.

Seite 55

Übung 13: 1. If Paul's mother hadn't been ill, his breakfast would have been ready. 2. If his bike hadn't had a puncture, he wouldn't have gone to school by bus. 3. If he hadn't taken the bus, he wouldn't have arrived at school too early. 4. If he hadn't prepared for the test, he couldn't/wouldn't have got all answers right. 5. If he had had money for milk, he would have bought some in the break. 6. If he hadn't left his books at school, he would have been able to do his homework. 7. If he hadn't had enough time, he wouldn't/couldn't have repaired his bike. 8. If he had been tired, he couldn't/wouldn't have watched the late movie.

Seite 57

Test 1: 1. will have to go, 2. were (was), 3. had not lost; would not have become, 4. would be able to see, 5. had woken up, 6. can ask, 7. would have enjoyed; had not drunk, 8. will see, 9. don't practise; will forget, 10. saved, 11. would be able to see, 12. were (was)

Seite 58

Test 2: If buffalo tongue hadn't been a great and expensive delicacy when sold in the butcher's shops in the Eastern States, hundreds of hunters wouldn't have come to shoot the animals. / If the USA hadn't been building a railroad to the Pacific, the railway company wouldn't have killed even more buffalo. / If at first the big steam engines hadn't made the Indians run away, they would have attacked the railroad. / If the Indians hadn't lost their fear, they wouldn't have attacked the railway. / If the white man hadn't destroyed the Indian way of life, the Indians wouldn't have been forced to spend their lives on reservations.

Seite 59

Test 3: 1. hits; will score, 2. doesn't hit; won't score, 3. will score; hits, 4. wants; must score, 5. doesn't score; can't win
Test 4: 1. when, 2. when, 3. If, 4. if, 5. when, 6. when, 7. If, 8. if

Seite 60

Test 5: 1. would not lend, 2. would you say, 3. would Jack have known, 4. were bitten, 5. would not have lost, 6. would have been hung, 7. would have had, 8. would have been, 9. had been

Seite 61

Test 6: 1. If you read pages 40–56, this exercise will be very easy for you. 2. If you waited for another 45 minutes, you could see the Changing of the Guard at Buckingham Palace. 3. If you went to New York, which sights would you like to see? 4. If the weather hadn't been so bad, I would have visited you yesterday. 5. I would have enjoyed the party more if Sandra had come. 6. If I am not tired this evening, I will go to a party with my friends. 7. If Boris Becker hadn't won Wimbledon, he would not have become so well-known.

Partizipien

Seite 63

Übung 1: 1. After serving/Having serviced his car last week, he drove … 2. Hearing the noise, she went to the window … 3. Paul fell and broke his leg trying to get off the bus. 4. Mary watched the policeman controlling the traffic. 5. After arriving/Having arrived home, Mrs Miller forgot … 6. He thanked the visitors for their interest in the exhibition after welcoming/having welcomed them. 7. MacCool damaged his car trying to park it.

Seite 65

Übung 2: 1. Having watched the late movie yesterday evening, MacCool went to bed early. 2. Although wearing white jeans, MacCool worked in the garden. 3. Leaning on the gate, George chatted to his friend. 4. Being new at school, Linda was shy. 5. Having won a million pounds, MacCool wants to buy a Ferrari. 6. When looking for a new cooker, come to our studios.

Seite 67

Übung 3: 1. The plane flying over us is not from LTU. 2. The candidates waiting for the test are very nervous. 3. The pilot acting very carefully changed the course. 4. Passengers travelling by ship should know how to use a life-jacket. 5. The man waiting for the boss is applying for a job. 6. The company producing those cars is based in Chicago. 7. The bobby telling Tom the right way is very friendly.

Seite 68

Übung 4: 1. Tourists taking their cars with them … 2. Whenever visiting her aunt, … 3. Having heard (After hearing) my side … 4. Although not having much money left, … 5. (When) Trying to learn his lessons … 6. Having done (After doing) his homework, … 7. (When) Turning on the lights, Peter is …

Übung 5: 1. Trains leaving this station take one hour to get to London. 2. Hearing the news, she hurries to her neighbour. 3. Sandra noticed a strange-looking man entering the restaurant. 4. After reading (Having read) the letter, he phoned his mother immediately. 5. Tourists travelling by plane shouldn't smoke.

Seite 69

Übung 6: 1. waiting, 2. finding, 3. wanting, 4. not wearing, 5. doing, 6. knowing, 7. preparing, 8. having, 9. working, 10. arriving

Seite 71

Übung 7: 1. Having been questioned by the police, Helen … 2. When told that there would be no test, MacCool … 3. Last week I read a book written by Karl May. 4. Scolded by her mother one hour ago, Sandra felt very sad. 5. If fired, Mr Miller will … 6. The TV set bought last week was out of order yesterday.

Seite 72

Übung 8: … two hours after the 100.000 pound ransom, paid by his father, the mayor of Nottingham, was … / The money, left at a restaurant … / The kidnapper's car, finally overtaken … / One kidnapper, thrown out of the car … / The second kidnapper, injured by the police, died later on. / The third escaped without the money left in the car. / Later the boy's father, Mr Owen, interviewed at his office in Nottingham by the press, said, … / … if I had not paid the money demanded by the gangsters?

Seite 73

Übung 9: 1. All people invited will come to the party. 2. All letters written today should be sent out tomorrow. 3. Yesterday I discovered a book written by my grandmother. 4. The car brought to the garage last monday has now been repaired. 5. Sandra eats a cake made by her mother. 6. The Titanic, built in 1911, wanted to cross the Atlantic Ocean faster than any ship before. 7. Martin Luther King, murdered in 1968, was one of the … 8. Robert Burnes, born in Scotland, is the Scottish national poet.

Seite 74

Test 1: 1. Yesterday Sam discovered a novel written by his grandfather. 2. My family moved to a house built in the 16th century. 3. Last night a policeman investigating a robbery was shot. 4. The student getting the highest marks will get a special prize. 5. The police car following the kidnappers hit an ambulance. 6. Tourists from outside Europe wanting to visit Great Britain must join a special queue at the passport control. 7. The robber caught by the police last night is a well-known member of the Crane Gang. 8. Look, there are some children running across the street without looking left or right. 9. Not being perfect, MacCool makes mistakes too.

Seite 75

Test 2: 1. sitting, 2. writing, 3. living, 4. helped, 5. needing, 6. flying, 7. taken, 8. Having lost, 9. written, 10. not built, 11. waiting, 12. standing

Abschlusstests

Seite 76

Test I: 1. Ein Nebensatz wird durch eine Konjunktion oder ein Relativpronomen eingeleitet. 2. Die Wortstellung ist: SPO (Subjekt, Prädikat, Objekt) 3. Gleichzeitigkeit, Vorzeitigkeit und Zukunftsbezug 4. Ein Nebensatz wird durch Komma abgetrennt, wenn er an erster Stelle steht. 5. where; somewhere; everywhere; wherever, 6. „da" und „seit", d. h. kausal und temporal. Beispiele: Since MacCool is ill, he isn't able to go to school (kausal). *oder* MacCool hasn't visited his aunt since last monday (temporal). 7. who, whom, which, that und whose 8. Der Relativsatz steht immer hinter dem Wort oder Satzteil, auf das/den er sich bezieht.

Seite 77

Test II: 1. If there were no frogs, there wouldn't be any storks. 2. If there weren't any storks, there wouldn't be any babies. 3. If there weren't any babies, there wouldn't be any Germans. 4. will/can make, 5. were (was), 6. would have visited, 7. had looked; wouldn't have been, 8. will (must) stay, 9. were/was fully booked, 10. must read

Seite 78/79

Test III: The British television service started in 1936 but it was closed down three years later when war broke out. It was not reopened until 1946. Television did not become a mass medium overnight. With a pre-war audience of about 20.000 homes in the London area, the service slowly extended to about 1.500.000 in 1952, covering England and Scotland. The Coronation of Queen Elizabeth II in 1953 increased the number of viewers considerably. About one million TV sets were bought in that year because many people wanted to see the broadcast of the ceremony, which was shown all over the world. In 1958 a second channel called Independent Television (ITV) was introduced. It was financed by advertising, while the BBC continued to be paid for by the licence fees which were collected from all owners of TV sets.

The new channel was so successful that from that time on the number of sets increased by about a million every year. If the new channel had not been introduced, British television would not have been so popular and successful. In the early 60s the BBC started another channel, BBC 2, and a greater variety of programmes were produced. Experiments with colour had been going on since the birth of television. In 1953 a satisfactory system which was developed in the USA was adopted in the USA and Japan. Willy Brandt gave a speech to open the first programme shown in colour in Germany.

Other countries adopted other systems, mainly the German PAL and the French SECAM system. Nowadays every household has a colour TV set. If the TV had not been invented, a lot of people would not have known what to do in their free time.

Seite 80

Test IV: 1. The whole world knows William Shakespeare, who wrote many plays. 2. Mary knows Mr Smith, whose book has been well received by the critics. 3. The big ship which sank on the way to America was the Titanic. 4. My neighbour, who does my garden, knows a lot about flowers. (*oder:* My neighbour, who knows a lot about flowers, does my garden.) 5. The music we listened to yesterday was by Michael Jackson. 6. The firm I warned you about is going bankrupt. 7. The bike you wanted me to buy was no good. 8. Liz Taylor, who acted in Caesar and Cleopatra, judged the competition. 9. This girl who tells you all about safety in a plane is a stewardess. 10. The book (which was) written by Tolstoi was very interesting. 11. Tim wants to meet Günter Grass, whose book has just been published. 12. The patient in room 12 wants to see his wife, who is in room 14. 13. The money mother looked for yesterday has been found. 14. That's the man whose wife sailed round the world single-handed. 15. All the work I've been helping Sandra with is done now. 16. who, 17. which, 18. which, 19. whose, 20. who, 21. kein Relativpronomen / that / which

Seite 81

Test V: 1. <u>After MacCool had come home yesterday</u>, he did the dishes. 2. <u>While grandfather was reading the newspaper</u>, the telephone rang. 3. <u>As MacCool had lost all his money</u>, he wasn't able to pay the bill. 4. Tim follows MacCool <u>everywhere he goes.</u> 5. <u>Since the weather is bad</u>, the children can't play outside. 6. MacCool is going to buy a new BMX bike <u>however much it costs.</u> 7. He plays football <u>like Pelé used to play.</u> 8. The girl married the man <u>although she didn't love him.</u> 9. <u>Because I haven't got any money</u>, I can't go on holiday this year. 10. Sam must run to school <u>because he has overslept this morning.</u> 11. <u>Although he overslept</u>, he arrived on time. 12. <u>Wherever he went</u>, MacCool took his book with him. 13. <u>After Frank Busemann had won a silver medal in Atlanta</u>, he was welcomed home in Recklinghausen. 14. The police followed the robber <u>everywhere he went.</u> 15. MacCool behaves <u>as if he doesn't speak English.</u>
Adverbialsatz der Zeit: 1, 2, 13
Adverbialsatz des Ortes: 4, 12, 14
Adverbialsatz des Grundes: 3, 5, 9, 10
Adverbialsatz des Gegensatzes: 6, 8, 11
Adverbialsatz der Art und Weise: 7, 15

Seite 82

Test VI: wanting/wanting/listening/built/called/discovering/expecting/living/helped/celebrating

Schulsorgen?

Neben dieser Buchreihe bietet die Schülerhilfe, Deutschlands große Nachhilfe-Organisation, einen regelmäßigen Förderunterricht. Dort gibt's qualifizierte Hausaufgaben-Betreuung in kleinen Gruppen und preiswerte Nachhilfe ab der Grundschule. Schülerhilfen finden Sie in vielen deutschen Städten.

Wählen Sie unsere bundeseinheitliche Telefon-Nr. 19418 montags bis freitags von 15.00 bis 17.30 Uhr.

(Ganztagsauskunft unter 0209/19 418)

Schülerhilfe

Lernen macht wieder Spaß